Ba Ye Zwa

the people live

Judy Seidman

South End Press

Boston   1978

Bertolt Brecht's "To Posterity," from *Bertolt Brecht, His Life, His Art ,His Times* by F. Ewen, published by Calder and Boyars Ltd. Reprinted by permission of the publisher.

"A Road Gang's Cry,"and "The Song of Sunrise" from *Sounds of a Cowhide Drum* by Oswald Mbuyiseni Mtshali published by Oxford University Press; ©Oswald Joseph Mtshali 1971. Reprinted by permission of the publisher.

"Somehow we survive" and "Return to us" from *A Simple Lust* by Dennis Brutus published by Heineman Educational Ltd.; © Dennis Brutus 1973. Published by permission of the author.

"Back of the Moon" from *King Kong* by Pat Williams and Ralph Trewhela published by Collins Publishers. Reprinted by permission of the publisher.

First Edition

Printed in the U.S.A. Copyrights are still required for book production in the U.S. However, in our case it is a disliked necessity. In regards to the written text of *Ba Ye Zwa*, any properly footnoted quotation of up to 250 sequential words may be used without permission. In regards to all the drawings in *Ba Ye Zwa*, written permission from the publisher is required for reproduction in any form or manner.

Library of Congress Catalog Card Number: 77-18421
ISBN 0-89608-002-1 paperback
      0-89608-003-1 hardcover
Published by:

South End Press, Box 68, Astor Station
Boston, Mass. 02123

to posterity

Truly, I live in dark times!
A guileless word is folly, A smooth forehead
Betokens insensitiveness, He who laughs
Has not yet heard
The terrible news.

Bertolt Brecht

acknowledgements

All books are to some extent a co-operative effort. This one particularly owes its existence to Gay and Neva Seidman for editing and lay-out, to Pat Walker and the South End Press, to my parents, to Neil Parsons for help with the history, and to my many friends in Southern Africa for their suggestions, contributions, and encouragement.

Swaziland, October 1977   J.S.

contents

Ba Ye Zwa

the people live

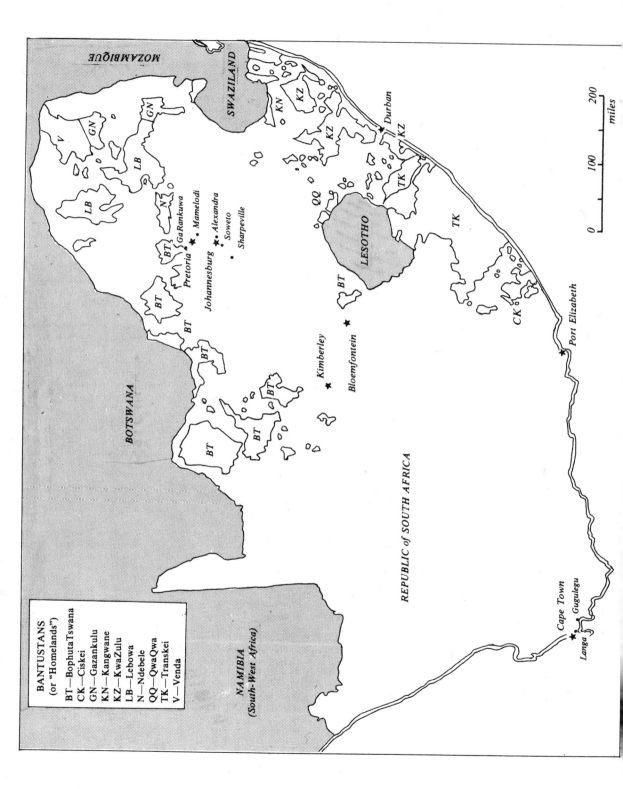

BANTUSTANS
(or "Homelands")

BT—BophutaTswana
CK—Ciskei
GN—Gazankulu
KN—Kangwane
KZ—KwaZulu
LB—Lebowa
N—Ndebele
QQ—QwaQwa
TK—Transkei
V—Venda

MOZAMBIQUE

SWAZILAND

Durban

KN

KZ

KZ

KZ

LESOTHO

TK

TK

LB

GN

V

GN

LB

N

GaRankuwa

Mamelodi

Pretoria

Alexandra

Johannesburg

Soweto

Sharpeville

BT

BT

QQ

BT

BT

BT

Kimberley

Bloemfontein

BT

BT

BT

CK

Port Elizabeth

BOTSWANA

REPUBLIC of SOUTH AFRICA

NAMIBIA
(South-West Africa)

Cape Town

Gugulegu

Langa

0   100   200

miles

Abantu ba ye zwa—The people live. They survive in conditions that barely provide physical necessities. And they transcend those conditions in kindness and love, in music and poetry, in hope and struggle. This is the story of the people of South Africa.

Imagine a society like nineteenth century England in the throes of the Industrial Revolution. Men doing the most back-breaking manual labor for ten or twelve hours a day. Villages and slums feeding the factories with laborers whose wages are so low that families starve. Child labor. A new upper class springing up with these factories. They build stately mansions, buy new clothes for every social event and have servants to wash and cook and garden.

Imagine a society where all the manual laborers are black, and the rulers are white. Unlike England, the rich in this society have a distinct advantage in their efforts to "keep the workers in their place." A mere glance will tell where a person belongs. The laborers live only in their allotted ghettos; they must get permission to travel; they are allowed only rudimentary education; they are exiled to distant reserves when they are no longer able to work.

This is precisely the situation in South Africa. The great majority of the working population is black. Every condition above applies—including children starving to death. Blacks must get permission to stay in an area or to travel. They receive very limited schooling, and when they are no longer able to work, they are shipped to barren lands that many of them have never seen before, and left to eke out a subsistence living from worn-out soil.

If a government uses color to determine each individual's social position, of course it will justify this with racist theories. But at heart apartheid is not simply race prejudice gone wild. It is a cruelly thorough method of maintaining an immoral and unjust social system.

The Cold Realities

Twenty-four million people live in the Republic of South Africa; of these one-fifth are white, four-fifths black. (But some organizations claim that the number of blacks has been consistently underestimated.)

A few South African racial categories:

White: Afrikaner or English, claiming European descent only. (Frequent intermarriage in the early days of colonization makes this something of a myth.)

Black: Any non-white (except **Honorary White**—dark-skinned visitors from overseas).

Asian: of Asian descent.

Coloured: of mixed descent.

African: of African descent (also "Bantu," an insulting corruption of the isiZulu word for "people").

The whites are the owners, the managers, the professionals, the foremen and skilled workers: the "baas" ("boss" in Afrikaans). Blacks are the laborers: farm hands, road crews, domestic servants, factory workers, miners. This is, of course, not an absolute division—there is a pitifully small group of black university lecturers, doctors, lawyers, school principals, a newspaper editor and a few journalists. But even these must fight a constant battle to keep their positions and the few privileges the law permits them.

This racial division is created and maintained by a government that is totally, self-consciously white. The three-quarters of the population that is black is not allowed to vote in national elections. This is not unofficial local custom or policy, as it was in the southern states of the United States. The national law of the Republic of South Africa explicitly denies the black majority the right to vote.

This white government uses all its powers—the law, the police and courts, the military, taxes, even social services—to structure society for its benefit.

> The fact of the matter is this: we need them (the blacks) because they work for us . . . but the fact that they work for us can never . . . entitle them to claim political rights.
> —*Prime Minister J.V. Vorster*[1]

And the whites enjoy the benefits. They have cars, servants, high social security, excellent medicine. They live in a cocoon of glassed-in apartments, super highways, carpeted farmhouses, department stores and swimming pools. America, Europe and Japan supply them with the latest gadgetry. In 1969, whites received an average per capita income, for every man, woman and child, of $109 per month, where blacks received $8 per month.[2] The poorer South African white owns only one car. The poorer black does not eat.

IT'S an unhappy phenomenon that as soon as the guarantees run out the TV set turns temperamental, the washing machine wanes or the pool pump peters out.

...Berange has introduced the country's first household maintenance scheme.

The nine most obvious appliances to be covered would include fridge, washing machine, stove, water geyser, polisher, vacuum, pool pump, hi-fi and TV set.

Citizen, Sept. 17, 1977

> Because of the high degree of consensus among the whites in favour of white supremacy, which reflects the material interests of the different white groups in its structure, conflicts among the whites is concerned essentially with the form that white supremacy should take...[3]

Apartheid (an Afrikaans word meaning separation, and pronounced, by odd coincidence, "apart-hate") is the political system that buttresses this division of society. According to apartheid theory, it is natural, necessary, and right.

A sign on a cafe on Caroline Street,
Hillbrow, Johannesburg(1976)

FOOD & FUN
WHITES
ONLY

Officially, the black majority in South Africa may only see this world as servants and laborers. They live in concrete boxes, tin shacks and mud huts, on a diet of "mealie" (corn) porridge, while their labor keeps white society alive.

Roadgang

the corroded surface must be broken
to reach the water piped underneath

humanity grows from cracked hands on an ax
man suspended between rise and crash
a concert of gut strings and steel
sweat

tear down and
rebuild the world

lift together smash
pause
lift together

J.S.

This division of labor—and race—can only survive while it is backed up by rigid control of the subject population. All blacks over the age of sixteen must carry a pass, or reference book, which gives the official version of the holder's life: a goverment-assigned number, birthplace, ethnic group. The area where he or she has official permission to live. A stamp showing occupation—renewed by the (white) employer each month. Any special permission to travel. Even a stamp giving official permission to look for work. These papers describe the boundaries of each individual's "freedom."

For blacks in South Africa, permission to live in an area does not depend upon their needs or their families' needs. According to

Once more it is the ordinary guys who get stopped and ordered to produce. The upper-crust types are never exposed to this terrible ordeal as most of them own cars.

It is the guy who walks the city street looking for a job. It is not the high-clan people. They are either working within the safe confines of their office or driving around town.

It is the breadwinner that is usually stopped and not the vandals, the won't works, who bask in the sun while we are working.

Not the vandal who breaks into people's houses while the owners are at work. The vandals who sleep during the day and at night rob people of their pay-packets.

Most vandals in the townships are 10(1)A's, and most won't works are able to smell a police van kilometres away.

Unbearable

But then, with the present political climate, do we need to have a more unbearable life than the one we are leading? It is such a pity that the people affected by this have nowhere to go.

If they did, they would also pack their bags, like so many of our intellectuals, for greener pastures. Then we would soon see what would happen to our industry. But then that's only wishful thinking.

Weekend World, May 1, 1977

official policy, it depends entirely on the demands and needs of white-controlled industry. A man often receives permission to live in an urban area while his wife and children must remain in a village hundreds of miles away.

The pass laws are so complex that many people knowingly or unknowingly violate some section of them. They must bribe petty officials in order to continue with everyday life. And people are always vulnerable to arrest and punishment. In one year, 1974, over half a million Africans were arrested in South Africa for "reference book and influx control offenses."[4] And in 1976, the fines for a simple pass offense doubled from R50 to R100 ($57 to $115)—a month's wages or more for most blacks. The alternative is jail.

THE ASSEMBLY — A total of 250 030 Africans —216 112 men and 33 918 women—were arrested in South Africa for reference book and influx control offences last year, Mr Jimmy Kruger, the Minister of police, revealed in the Assembly yesterday.

The biggest number of arrests were in Johannesburg, 53 169 men and 5 919 women; followed by Pretoria, 40 528 men and 5 919 women; the East Rand, 40 737 men and 4 359 women; the West Rand, 14 069 men and 3 467 women; the Cape Peninsula, 12 074 men and 4 025 women; and Durban, 6 147 men and 565 women. — Sapa.

Rand Daily Mail
extra, March 5, 1977

Black people in South Africa are not allowed to move around the country. Laws say where they must live and work. These are the Pass Laws. Pass Laws control the lives of every family. Until the Pass Laws change, you should understand how they work. Then you can avoid some of the troubles they cause.

The government of South Africa controls where people can live and work. They do this with Reference Books. Every black person carries a Reference Book. Reference Books are stamped to show where the person can work. These stamps show when someone has permission to be in a place. For example, if you live and work in Johannesburg, your book must be stamped to show you have permission. If there is no stamp in your book you can be arrested. Many people are arrested every year because of the Pass Laws. Try and get the right stamp in your child's book to prevent this happening.

The new Reference Book your child gets will not have any stamps. The first thing your child must do after he collects his book is to get his stamps.

The Pass Laws say that all people living in the urban (town) areas must work. Men between the ages of 15 and 65 should be employed. So must women between the ages of 15 and 60. But women who are housewives do not have to get paid employment.

There are different kinds of stamps about employment. Here is a list of the kinds of stamps you can get. This is for people living in the urban areas.
- a Scholar's Permit
- a Work Seeker's Stamp
- Registration in employment
- a stamp to show you are self-employed...

Registration in Employment: People who have jobs must be registered. The Labour Office will stamp your book. If you are a man, your employer must sign the book every month. For women, the book is only signed when they start a job...

Your child must have one of these stamps in his book. If he stays in an urban area without one of these stamps, he can be arrested. He might be sent away to a special school...

Sometimes stamps have dates on them. Always check what day the stamp ends. This is the day stamped in the book. After this date the stamp is no longer good.

A Scholar's Permit may run out at the end of the year. If your child is still in school the next year, get another stamp put in the book.

A work seeker's stamp will always have a date on. After the date on the stamp has passed, it is the same as having no stamp. Your child may be arrested.

If your child does not find work before this date, he must go back to the Labour Office. He must get another stamp.

When your child finds a job he must get a letter from his employer. Then he should take the letter to the Labour Office. The Labour Office will stamp his book to show he is working. This stamp lasts as long as your child works in that job...

Sometimes the Labour Office puts a stamp in a book which says the person must leave the area.

This stamp uses the following words: "Ordered to leave the prescribed area within 72 hours." The Labour Officer uses this stamp to endorse someone out of an area...

"Child Care," Lesson 9, People's College, Weekend World, May 1, 1977

At the moment urban Africans may move from one town to another only if both towns fall under the jurisdiction of the same Bantu Administration Board.

There are twenty-two administration boards.

Rand Daily Mail extra,
Feb. 4, 1977

The law controls where you live and work; it also controls what work you may do. Skilled jobs are often restricted to whites.

SIR, — I wonder how long we Blacks must suffer?

Bantu Education officials are busy establishing technical training schools so that Blacks can be trained as technicians.

I'm sure all Blacks appreciate that.

But where things begin to go wrong is when we have completed our training and are fully qualified.

It is with tremendous difficulty that we can find jobs. All sorts of White-made laws prevent Black men from working as mechanics or brick-layers, for example.

So a fully qualified mechanic ends up working as a "garage assistant" with a wage far below that of the White man with similar qualifications.

South Africa needs qualified workers so give us a chance. If we can do it, let us do it and pay us for it.

ERIC NDLELA
Johannesburg
World, April 21, 1977

SITUATIONS VACANT

EXPERIENCED COOK/HOUSEKEEPER
Johannesburg pass. Good wages. Live in.
Telephone 40-6591 or call 167 Corlett Drive,
Bramley.

HOUSEMAID/COOK
Aged 30-40 years. Live in. Must be experienced with children. Must have Benoni pass.
Telephone 836-2231 Ext. 18 during office
hours. 849-7965 after 6 p.m.

DOMESTIC MAID
Conscientious with references. Registered
for Kempton Park. To commence
immediately. Tel. 975-7742

EXPERIENCED COOK HOUSEMAID
Required immediately. Top salary. Apply
with references to 25 Tottenham Ave.,
Melrose. Tel. 42-5950

EXPERIENCED HOUSE/GARDENER
With recent references and up to date pass.
Apply 45 Alexandra Avenue, Craighall.

EXPERIENCED HOUSE/COOK MAID
To sleep in. JHB pass only need apply, 9
Rathmines Road, Highlands North, JHB

EXPERIENCED JEWISH COOKING
Puddings and able to bake well. Sleep in.
Must produce references with JHB pass.
Apply after 6 p.m. 21 Darwin Avenue, Savoy
Estates.

EXPERIENCED machinist with excellent
references wanted for dressmaker. Call 36
Krause Street, Vrededorp.

GENERAL HOUSEMAID
With Johannesburg pass for Highlands
North. Telephone 786-1776

GENERAL HOUSEMAID/NAN
With Johannesburg pass required. Live in.
Apply 124 8th Road, Kew.

HOUSEMAID/NANNY/COOK
Coloured or Black required for Benoni area.
Live in. Telephone 54-7843

MAID REQUIRED
JHB PASS. 111 Buckingham Avenue,
Craighall, telephone 22-5021

MIDDLEAGED DOMESTIC
Wanted to work in Fourways. Must have
Sandton pass and contactable references.
Phone office hours 724-5543 ask for Mrs
Misdorp

PART-TIME MAID
For serviced flat. One person. Own room
and bed provided. Plain cooking. Good
ironer. R30 monthly. Apply Monday or

Your pass tells you what
jobs you may apply to,
and in which areas.

What does this mean, for instance, to a housemaid? She lives in the black township with her family, takes a bus to work at 4:30 or 5 in the morning, and gets home again at 8 or 9 at night. Or she lives in the "servant's quarters" attached to the white house, separated from her husband, children and friends, permanently at the service of "Madam."

Service

Suburban house among the leaves
carpets and a silver tea service—
a kindly, godly couple.
Saying casually to an elderly maid,
Tea at sixthirty, Esther.

Which means she rises at five-thirty, six
to turn on the kettle
to bring them tea in bed.
(It's just past nine when this is said.)

She sleeps alone in a room attached
her papers are in order.
Her children live (illegally)
with a sister in Dube.
She sees them on her day off
(—she has most Sundays,
they are a kindly, godly couple).

Esther has been with us forever—we
could not live without her.

So many kindnesses a silver tea service
permits.

J.S. '75

Can you blame Madam? She merely complies with the law. The maid's family is not allowed to live in a "white" area. Should Madam not live up to the position society has given her?

This is true for all those who participate in South African society. They merely follow the law. When Ford or General Motors, Kelloggs or General Electric, build a plant in South Africa, they are required to hire whites in the management positions. They pay their black workers less than whites, and the government stops them from bargaining with African trade unions. Of course, all these laws ensure higher profits for the companies—and are they not in the business to make profits?

The average world rate [of return on investment] during 1960-70 was 11 per cent, but capital invested in South Africa earned a phenomenal 18.6 per cent.[5]

These investments boost the whole economic system upon which apartheid thrives. Multinational corporations based in Europe and United States shore up the apartheid economy directly by building factories. And more and more they support it by lending money to the white minority regime. In November 1976, for example, Citibank of New York loaned the South African government $110 million.[6]

The multinationals claim that simply because they are so involved with South Africa, they can try to influence the regime, persuade it to mend its ways. They say apartheid—which provides such cheap labor for their factories—does not sit easily on their corporate consciences. About 30 U.S. companies have signed a "manifesto," pledging themselves to provide equal employment opportunities—but the South African *Financial Mail* has disputed its real effectiveness.

The American business manifesto needs to go a lot further. And be followed up with determination.

Two main points must be made about the manifesto. The first is that it is more significant for what it leaves out than for what it says. The second is that signing statements of principle, however worthy, on one side of the Atlantic is one thing; putting them into practice on the other is another...

The most obvious omission is the question of trade union rights for Africans. Not only does continuing refusal by US (and other) companies to recognise African unions constitute a perpetuation of racial discrimination. Equally important, many of the problems the manifesto seeks to tackle arise in large part from the fact that Africans are denied collective bargaining rights...

The other glaring omission is that the manifesto is (deliberately?) evasive on the whole question of the industrial colour bar where it counts most—ie on the shop-floor. This is a veritable minefield of complexities.

The second aspect of the manifesto is the need to give it teeth. American parent companies should take a much closer interest in the *everyday* operations of their SA subsidiaries than they have done up till now...

There is a genuine question in Washington as to whether the recent anti-apartheid gesture by the US firms was aimed more at the White House and liberal American stockholder groups than at the Vorster government and its policies. As a head-on confrontation with the broader policies of SA apartheid, it is just not on.

"If you mean do we envision our plant managers going to jail or us breaking the laws of SA, no we do not," Charles McCabe of General Motors told the *FM* in New York shortly after the programme was announced.

"We endorse the programme. We will work for equitable conditions there, and have already done so for some time. But where our work conflicts with existing SA law we will work within the proper channels to change the law."

Spokesmen for IBM and the 11 other signatories to the pledge, echoed those sentiments.

Spokesmen for the signatory firms were emphatic that their statement of principles is in no way a threat to pull out their substantial investments in SA. Moreover the companies plan, their officials say, to continue their investment plans in the country, and that there is no hard deadline for the implementation of all six points.

Financial Mail, March 4, 1977

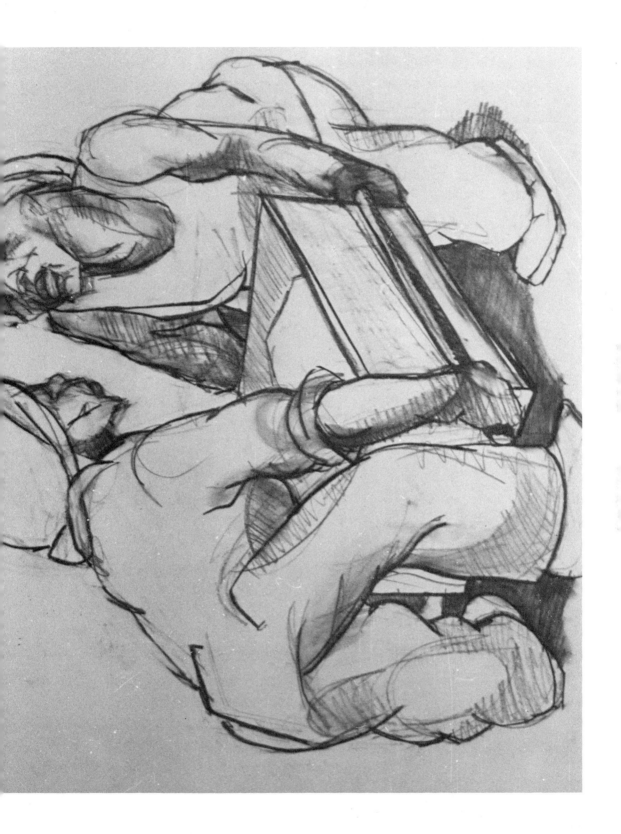

If the rulers of South Africa dictate where, when and how blacks work, it is not surprising that they also dictate wages. Black trade unions are not recognized. Africans may be "represented" to management by a works committee, which can only advise. There is no recourse: before 1973 all strikes by blacks were illegal; since then, they are only practically illegal. (Only one strike by Africans since then has fulfilled the restrictions of the law.)

Strikes and trade unions for blacks still spring up. The South African government attempts to suppress them as dangerous to the public welfare.

In 1946, memorable moment, upwards of 100,000 "mine boys" came out on strike ... thousands of them left their compounds one day and began to march to neighboring Johannesburg. They marched with no intention other than that of asking for passes to return home to their families. They were exercising the traditional right of withdrawing their labour, the one contingency with which the Chamber [of Mines] is not fully equipped to deal. But on their way to Johannesburg they were met by the police, and the police bludgeoned and battered them back to their compounds, while the press of white South Africa and every tuppeny politician shouted rape and murder. Some were killed. Hundreds were admitted to hospital. On other parts of the Rand "mine boys" who wished to join this strike—which caught both Government and mining companies, who believed it "could not happen," utterly unprepared—were forced to go down the pits, whereupon they struck by refusing to come up again. They were driven to the surface by the police—and the words are those of the Rand Daily Mail at the time—"stope by stope and level by level." All their officials were arrested and documents seized...[7]

So the workers get the barest minimum wage necessary for sur-
vival...usually.

THE main grievance of African workers in the Cape Town area is low wages—a survey has revealed that 50 per cent earn less than R25 a week (or R107,50 a month).

The survey shows:

•Wages in dairy and security firms are particularly low, averaging R17 and R20 a week.

•State, provincial and municipal workers do not have better wages, except a few highly-paid workers in State employ. The average for all three groups is R23 a week.

•Averages in the building industry, iron and steel manufacturing and baking and confectionary were R27 a week.

•Workers in commercial and distributive trades and stevedores earned the highest wages, according to the survey— R32 and R36 a week.

The survey by two University of Cape Town lecturers, Janet Graaf and Johan Maree, is the first of its kind for 20 years in Cape Town...

The survey shows that a worker's legal status— under influx control regulations—determines his job and earning power. Earnings of migrant workers are less than those of resident workers.

About low wages, workers complained they could not keep up with the rise in the cost of living.

Rand Dail Mail extra, Nov. 11, 1976

In May 1976, the Poverty Datum Line—the estimated minimum amount of money a family must earn "in order to survive"—stood at $148.75 a month for a family of five in Soweto. To survive on the PDL, you spend almost three quarters of your money on food. You have no allowances for furniture or household utensils, doctors' bills or education, or other frills. Yet when this minimum for survival stood at $148.35 a month, the *average* income of an African family was only $84.[8]

For the people trapped in this legal and economic web, life offers few luxuries.

A typical resident is Mr Andreas Zungu, 32, who mixes concrete for Savage and Lovemore. He is a contract worker with a wife and three children back home. With overtime, working a six-day week from 6 am to 6 pm each day he earns R30 a week.

His biggest expenditure is on sorghum beer—R5 a week. For food he buys a R2,60 bag of potatoes every fortnight and a 15 cent tin of fish every day. He says he cannot afford meat at current prices—it may be that he cannot bother cooking meat after a day's work.

He spends 50 cents a week on drycleaning and a moderate amount each month on clothing. Andreas Zungu tries to send at least R20 home each week. Sometimes he is able to send his whole wage home.

His recreation is to talk to his mates and to drink with them at weekends. Sometimes he plays soccer.

Rand Daily Mail extra,
Oct. 16, 1975

Those who cannot find a place in industry may try agriculture. Two million blacks work on white-owned farms. The conditions there are worse than in the townships.

The director of the South African Agricultural Union [the white farm owners' organization] Mr Chris Cilliers, said farm workers earned good wages in South Africa.

He was not aware of any farmers who paid their workers only R5 [$6] a month, but if there were such cases they were "not representative".

Farmers in the Free State pay their workers an average of R12 to R20 [$14-$23] a month, while those with heavy vehicle licences earn about R25 [$29] and more.

Rand Daily Mail extra,
January 19, 1977

...   The labourers, who were recruited from Bronkhorstspuit in the Eastern Transvaal, were middle-aged women and children whose ages ranged between 10 and 13.

The farmer, a Mr. Meyer, said he gave his employees enough food to eat and a place to sleep. He confirmed that he paid each of his employees R5 a week. They slept on sacks spread on the ground, covered with blankets they carried from their homes when they were recruited.

Rand Daily Mail extra, Nov. 8, 1975

You work, and then one day you get the sack.

Mr Robert Tapulo Sekalane, 65, told me he had been employed with the firm for 30 years, and during that period had worked a 6 am to 6 pm day seven days a week.

His job was to look after cattle before slaughter, and his earnings when laid off were R35 a week.

Mr Sekalane is married with five children, all boys, of whom four are still in school. His wife lives on a small property at Matatiele in Transkei while Mr Sekalane has been sharing a rented room with one son in Alexandra Township.

He says he will have to return to his home and live out his days there. He has no savings, and was accustomed to sending R10 to R20 a week home to his wife from his pay packet.

"My heart is very sore about this thing. I did expect the firm to do something when I left. I am a Black man and have no power to make them do so."

Rand Daily Mail extra, April 8, 1977

A Roadgang's Cry

Pneumatic drills
roar like guns in a battlefield
as they tear the street.

Puffing machines swallow the red soil
and spit it out like a tuberculotic's sputum.

Business-bent brokers hurry past;
Women shoppers shamble tiredly, shooing their children;
Stragglers stop to stare
as the ruddy-faced foreman watches men
lifting a sewerage pipe into a trench.

It starts
as a murmur
from one mouth to another
in a rhythm of ribaldry
that rises to a crescendo
"Abelungu ngo'dam
Basibiza ngo Jim—
Whites are damned
they call us Jim."

Oswald Mbuyiseni Mtshali

Can one ask the government, politely, to give up its control? Can one ask the whites to give up their standard of living? Or the multinationals to share their profits with their black workers?

THE Prime Minister, Mr Vorster, last night gave a firm warning that the Government would not yield from its policy in several crucial areas.

There would be no yielding on the "right of our White people to retain control of their own destiny, the maintenance of law and order, and the determination of the kind of economic system under which we are to live and work," he said.

Mr Vorster was speaking to members of the Association of Chambers of Commerce.

He said all racial groups would be included in the economic mainstream "up to a point."

Weekend World,
April 17, 1977

Passes and job restrictions are the parameters, the cold regulations that structure the lives of black South Africans. Within these boundaries lie even colder realities: the size of your house, when you get up in the morning, the day-to-day grittiness of the struggle to make do.

Take your house. If you are black, you can only live in certain areas, fenced off from the cities—the "townships." Soweto. Alexandria. Guguletu. Langa. Only a handful of township houses have electricity, or a telephone, or even running water. There are no paved roads or street lighting.

But these are not villages: Soweto holds at least a million, perhaps a million and a half people. But the government officially recognizes only 700,000 people as living there. There are 96,000 houses—an official average of 8.8 people in a two, three or four room house. Unofficially, there are perhaps as many as 15 people per house. No new houses have been planned since 1970, because government policy disapproves of black families living in urban areas.[10]

The inhabitants of Soweto are housed in 96 000 houses, mostly four-roomed, with others of two, three and five rooms. All are of the same pattern, which catches the eye because the land where they stand is flat and barren. They have a dull colour, and as a result Soweto has an unfortunate image of dullness and monotony.

Most houses use candles, paraffin and a small group have gas. Most stoves operate on coal, and the layer of smog which covers Soweto for an hour or two from about 5.30 a.m. in the winter is both depressing and dangerous to traffic and health. Most toilets in Soweto are outside. Most houses have their taps in the yard.

Accommodation in Soweto is a major concern. Overcrowding is part and parcel of life in this community. Some of the houses which are so orderly and clean during the day, because the rooms are so small and the families large, have every available space in the house used as a bedroom in the night. One room is both a living room and bedroom, the kitchen is also a dining room, bedroom, pantry and bathroom.

Ellen Kuzwayo, Black Sash, Nov. 1975

In the township, you can almost never own your house. Instead, you must rent a standard model from the government. Any improvements such as electricity or piped-in water are, of course, at your own expense.

After the 1976 riots, the government decided to sell these same houses to their occupants (at 100 per cent profit). The houses went on sale for $2300, a lump sum beyond the resources of most blacks. The alternative was monthly installments of $21 for ten years. If you miss an installment, you may lose the house. And since you only live in the township on government sufferance, you have no security—you may be forced to move to a "homeland" even if you own your house outright. The plan has not been wildly successful.[11]

Most of the townships are miles outside the "white" cities where the township residents work. They must commute as many as three hours each way. If you must be at work by 7:30 a.m., you catch a bus or train at 5:30, jammed almost beyond endurance, and pay from your meager wages for the privilege.

Again, **I believe we should not perpetrate the sin that is Soweto.** God! it is enough that our Black bodies throttle each other out of life in this sinful cauldron called Soweto. I don't think we should speak of "improving the lot of the people of Soweto." **Hell can never be improved.**

Sketsh magazine, summer 1975
editorial

The most common type of house in Soweto is the 51/6. Although there are several variations on the standard model, it is basically a four-room house (with one room serving as the kitchen and another as a living-cum-bedroom).

Further details of the 51/6 include:

•Steel outside doors but no internal doors

•Outside WC

•Corrugated iron or asbestos roof; no ceilings

•Cement floors

•Windows in every room

•No stove, basin or running water in kitchen. Tenants expected to install them at their own cost. No hot water unless house electrified (installment cost paid by tenant).

•Size: Stand—12 m by 22 m (40 x 70 feet). Rooms—length and breadth varies from about 3 m to about 4 m (9 ft 6 inches x 12 ft 6 inches)...

Another prototype model house in Soweto is the 51/9, an improved version of the 51/6. The improvement consists of an internal bathroom and lavatory (although the "de luxe" version has five rooms instead of four).

Rand Daily Mail
May 2, 1977

The Dlaminis are an ordinary family—there are 12 of them, father, mother and 10.

Joseph Dlamini, 45, earns R100 a month as an Iscor worker, one son Wilfred, 23, earns R30 per month as a gardener and Obed, 20, earns R60 as a labourer...

The Dlaminis live in a four-room township home for R4,78 per month. Nearly everybody in the township, housing 80 000, live in the same houses, two small bedrooms, a kitchen and a dining room.

The Dlaminis have one item of furniture which they regard as grand—a hifi set still being paid on hire-purchase. For the rest, there is a home-made deal table, old chairs, and old beds for the whole family.

There are six school-going children in this family. Fees, books and uniforms cost the Dlaminis about R12 a month.

Basic costs to the Dlaminis on their income of R190 a month are: rent R4,78, food R72, coal R13,20, wood R1,80, bus transport (old rates) R11,70, school costs R12— total, R115,48.

The Dlaminis eat meat twice a week at a cost of R3 a week.

Rand Daily Mail, Oct. 15, 1977

The lucky ones live in government houses. The alternatives are less attractive. A man can live in a single-sex dormitory, separated from wife and children, crowded between high-rise concrete walls, with no privacy.

... The study details migrant worker accommodation in the townships of Langa, Nyanga and Guguletu—all areas of recent conflict—as well as accommodation outside the townships. It points out that besides the nearly 40 000 men living in single quarters there are an estimated 100 000 Africans living illegally in the townships.

With very few exceptions the study shows all facilities and accommodation are substandard.

Examples of the findings were:
•The main barracks at Langa were built in 1927/28. They house 2 032 men with 24 men in each room.

The Bantu Administration Board-run hostels are "dark, often dirty and morbidly depressing." There are no ceilings, no covering on brick floors, no lockers, no wall plugs. There is one bare electric light in each room.
•There are 44 dormitories and sheds provided by private companies for 3 472 workers. Most house 42-50 men in each. The men sleep in double bunks and there are no dividing walls between beds. In many cases the workers use cardboard to keep out the wind and for privacy. The only heating in dormitories is a central coal stove. The sheds have no heating.
•Employers have provided only about one lavatory for every 19 men and one shower for every 20...
•The Nyanga employers hostel and temporary sheds (built in 1968) together house nearly 3 500 men and have roofs that leak through the summer. The sheds are not raised above the ground and mud and water are carried into them in the rainy season.

There are no kitchen facilities whatever. Outside each hostel there is one tap and there are virtually no showers. On average 60 people do all their toiletries, cooking and washing with two toilets and two cold water taps.

Rand Daily Mail,
Jan. 15, 1977

And there are the real slums, shacks of tin and wood, tied together, with no sanitary facilities and water, except when it rains and comes in through the roof. These shacks are liable to be torn down at any moment at government expense. The officially-approved houses have long waiting lists for would-be residents.

SOME Johannesburg Coloured families have lived as squatters for more than 25 years in the notorious Kliptown ghetto.

As we inspected hovel after hovel, a Coloured community leader said: "The people are desperate and angry. You can see that for yourselves."

Mr Albie Pop, a school principal and elected representative of Kliptown, Nancefield and Eldorado Park on the Coloured Management Committee, warned: "This area could become the next South African flashpoint if action isn't taken soon to house these people properly. In the squatters' minds the limit has been reached."

A deputation led by Mr David Curry, deputy leader of the Labour Party, expected to meet three Cabinet Ministers on the issue next week, he said.

"If this was an earthquake zone hundreds of adequate temporary homes would have been built by now. The problem is that in the minds of the authorities squalor and poverty have become an accepted lifestyle for many Blacks," said Mr Pop.

Kliptown's two emergency camps were full, Mr Pop said. There were between 200 and 300 people living below the breadline with inadequate housing and no hope of re-settlement.

One squatter, Mrs Constance Sauls, 53, mother of eight, said: "I have lived in this place for 25 years. Others have been here longer. The schoolchildren in this pondokkie are suffering because there are 13 people under this roof."

Seven were schoolchildren. There was no electric light. They did their homework by candlelight amid the babble of adult conversation.

One bucket enclosed with corrugated iron strips, placed in the veld, was the toilet for the inhabitants of four pondokkies—more than three dozen people.

"Rats and leaking roofs are two of our big problems," a middle-aged squatter said.

Rand Daily Mail, March 10, 1977

The Song of Sunrise

The sword of daybreak
snips the shroud
of the night from the sky
and the morning
peeps through the blankets
like a baby rising
from its cot
to listen to the
peal of the bell.

Arise! Arise!
All workers!
To work! To work!
You must go!

Busses rumble,
Trains rattle,
Taxis hoot.

I shuffle in the queue
with feet that patter
on the station platform,
and stumble into the coach
that squeezes me like a lemon
of all the juice of my life.

Oswald Mbuyiseni Mtshali

EVEN the long-standing railway enthusiasts and transport experts gasped when South African Railways' planning engineer, Mr Jack Lloyd, revealed how crowded Soweto's trains actually are.

Addressing members of the Railway Society of Southern Africa in Johannesburg this week he illustrated his point by explaining that the SAR was having problems with damage to the battery boxes which are suspended beneath the coaches.

"We couldn't understand what was causing it," he said. "It was only after we had done some tests in the workshops that we realised the coaches were packed so full that the frames were actually sagging under the weight...causing the battery boxes to touch the rails."

Rand Daily Mail extra, May 14, 1976

The government controls your work and your living conditions, and it controls how you relax.

Recreation is controlled directly through "Whites Only" signs on theaters, parks, restaurants—even where blacks could afford to go to them. (Sometimes, as at the Rand Show in 1977, they take down the signs as a gesture to liberal opinion. But they retain the strict separation of facilities with more insult, because people think there has been a change and must be told where they belong.)

The government does provide blacks with one particular form of relaxation—liquor. The Bantu Affairs Department (the all-white government body in charge of blacks) builds and maintains liquor stores and large beerhalls in the townships. (Small black-owned drinking establishments, frequently with home-made liquor, thrive also, illegally.) Liquor is a major source of goverment revenue. If you can't give them bread and circuses, you can always try to get them drunk.

IT'S a curious commentary on official thinking that the West Rand Administration Board has spent nearly eight times as much—R31 126 —on rebuilding riot-damaged bottle stores and beer halls than the R3 995 it has on rebuilding schools. There is obviously something wrong with a scale of values which permits such a situation to occur, given the known housing shortage.

Yet Wrab is merely giving tortured expression to its nature. The lack of proper home ownership and business rights in the townships forces Wrab to depend heavily on liquor sales to finance itself. Its last budget provided for some 20 per cent of its income to come from this quarter.

With such dependence Wrab falls easily into the trap of wanting to have as high a sale as possible, whatever the destructive social consequences. That is recognised, and resented, by township residents and resulted in liquor outlets being particular targets for angry crowds last year.

Rand Daily Mail, April 5, 1977

For a moment as I looked at those young men around me, the luxury of a mild flood of conscience swept over me. They had all at one time or other had visions: to escape their environment; to oppose and overcome their context; to evade and out-distance their destiny by hard work and sacrifice, by education and native ability, by snatching from the table of occupation some crumbs of high-chaired culture. Lord, it struck me, what a treasury of talent I had here in front of me. Must they bury their lives with mine like this under a load of Sophiatown bottles?

Can Themba, The Will To Die

The government liquor establishments make no efforts to turn drinking into a social occasion. The beerhalls they build are concrete hangers with benches. Women are usually barred.

SIR — It is rather shocking to hear that in Atteridgeville women are allowed to sit and drink side by side with men in beerhalls.

It is true of course that women are capable of doing anything a man can do, but heavens, this does not mean they should compete with men in things such as sharing beerhalls.

They can at least drink at gatherings, or by themselves to relieve a hard day's tension.

My Lord! Not in beerhalls; look at the men who go there, most of them have no respect for each other. With women joining them, I shudder to think what kind of mothers are we going to have...

THOMAS KONAITE
Saulsville
World, April 1977

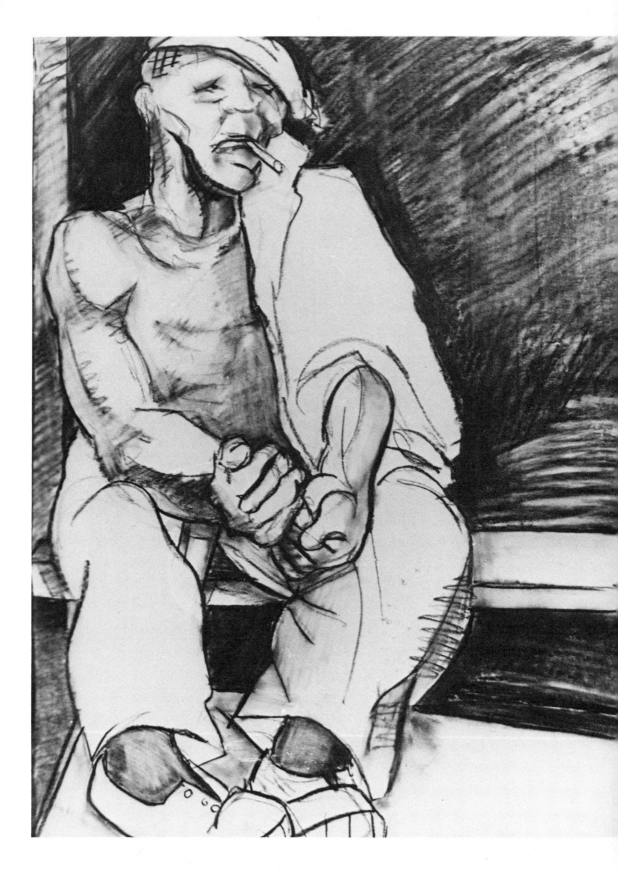

Living like this, what is there to hope for?

Dreams

Once you saw
Mercedes black gleams
Rows of books and magazines
High heels and whiskey and soda

Now only jagged shards
The water spilt
Across the worn-out earth.

J.S.

The People's Culture

In spite of all this, the African people have developed a culture and consciousness of their own. Common roots and experiences have created a common awareness; the people have built new foundations.

The townships have their own slang, hair styles, music, dance, art and poetry. They have institutions of their own, churches and bars, student movements and football associations, Drum magazine and the Black People's Convention. Where does self-reliance stop and politics begin?

For the most part, white society ignores these. African history is never taught in schools. Traditional African art and music are dubbed "tribal" or "primitive"; they are never the conscious creation of an artist working with symbols and experiences from his or her own life. Political and consciousness-raising organizations are always blamed on outside agitation, usually sinister.

A Johannesburg African, Solomon Linde, composed a song called "Wimoweh" which when recorded by a group of singers in the U.S.A. became a real hit and sold about 200,000 records. Linde got nothing at all until the Union [of South African Artists] ... made representations on his behalf and got L125 [$500] for him as "compensation."

Outlook, January 1955[12]

Love, kindness, even happiness still grow between the cracks in the surface of apartheid.

Somehow we survive
and tenderness, frustrated, does not wither.

Investigating searchlights rake
our naked unprotected contours;

over our heads the monolithic decalogue
of fascist prohibition glowers
and teeters for a catastrophic fall;

boots club the peeling door.

But somehow we survive
severance, deprivation, loss.

Patrols uncoil along the asphalt dark
hissing their menace to our lives,

most cruel, all our land is scarred with terror,
rendered unlovely and unloveable;
sundered are we and all our passionate surrender

but somehow tenderness survives.

Denis Brutus

A life is lived out on many levels. You live under apartheid with your family, in tin shacks yet among dreams and memories.

Return to us

when the sunset smoulders on the smooth horizon,
when the trees are starkly black
and beautiful
against the red and mauve of the sky

Return to us

when woodsmoke comes sweet and poignant
from the fields at dusk
after the winds of our fury have breathed
on the smouldering coals of our anger
and our fierce destruction has raged

O great patient enduring spirit
return to us

Dennis Brutus

People still survive, love and create. And out of this grow cultural and social patterns, transcending the material conditions that grind people down.

The traditions of the past shoot up into the present, transformed and adapted by new needs.

Take the idea of rain for the Tswana people. They lived on the edge of the Kalahari desert. Rain was crucial to life.

Apula ene, apula ene
Kana molongwaga retlatswalang
ge pula esane retlajang?

Let it rain, let it rain
for what shall we wear this year
if it doesn't rain what shall we eat?

Issac Schapera, Rain-making

When Christianity was introduced, the word "holy" was translated into seTswana as "boitshepo," a word describing the smell of the earth just after the rain, fresh and alive.

Today, the word for rain has several uses. *Pula* is rain. *Pu-pu-pu-pula* is a cheer, like "hip-hip-hurrah," suitable for football matches and political rallies. And in the Republic of Botswana, the currency is called *Pula*, and one Pula equals one South African Rand.

The history of a people has a concrete impact on their attitudes. A century ago, whites did not govern all of South Africa. Famous kings ruled, among them Shaka Zulu and Sekhukuni. Queen MaNtatisi took up arms for her people. There were independent farming communities, city states and trading systems. There were philosophies and arts. White rule could only be imposed by suppressing them. Even today they are not forgotten, but survive in words, songs and customs.

At two p.m. we came within sight of extensive cornfields, in a plain of great length, but not above two or three miles broad. In a short time part of the long-desired city was seen, standing on top of one of the highest hills in that part of Africa.

From this spot we were able to obtain a good view of the place, and were surprised at its extent. Every house was surrounded, at a convenient distance, by a good circular stone wall. Some of them were plastered on the outside and painted yellow. One we observed painted red and yellow, with some taste. The yard within the inclosure belonging to each house was laid with clay, made as level as a floor, and swept clean, which made it look neat and comfortable...

In some houses there were figures, pillars, etc. carved or moulded in clay, and painted with different colours, that would not have disgraced European workmen. They are indeed an ingenious people. We saw among them various vessels formed of clay, painted of different colours, and glazed, for holding water, milk, food and a kind of beer made from corn. They had also pots of clay, of all sizes, and very strong. Every part of their houses and yards is kept very clean. They smelt both iron and copper.

...At one place we stopped a short time with a blacksmith, who was making a pick-ax. He had three in hand, which were nearly finished; an assistant was employed to blow the bellows. A hard flint-stone served for his anvil, but he had a hammer with an iron head and a wooden handle, resembling the blacksmith's small ore-hammer in England.

Description of the city of Kurreechane, near modern Zeerust, South Africa, by J. Campbell in 1820.[13]

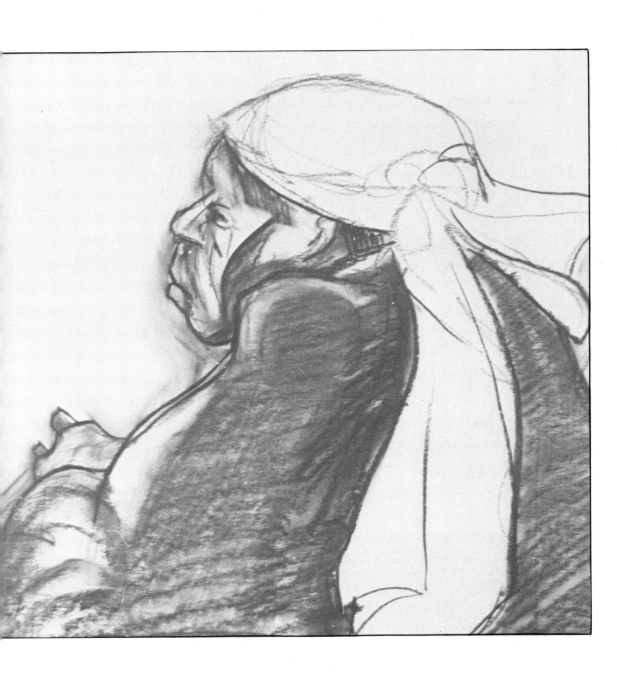

Africans have been independent and self-sufficient in the past. Must they accept this subjugation now?

Today's black townships have generated their own institutions, places where, at least for one night, people can be free.

Back of the Moon

Like paper riding in the breeze,
Like penny whistle melodies,
Like birds that fly across the sky
They know...
People can feel free as these
People being what they please
Being free and easy ... letting go ... *letting go*
LETTING GO!

Back of the Moon, boys,
Back of the Moon, boys,
Top shebeen* in Jo'burg is the Back of the Moon;
Better than night clubs,
Better than white clubs,
Right in front is the Back of the Moon!

Though the floor starts shaking when the place gets packed,
Chairs are breaking and the glasses cracked,
The night is in front and the day behind,
The Back of the Moon is where the folks unwind...

Back of the Moon, boys,
Back of the Moon, boys,
Right behind the shanties is the Back of the Moon
Back of the shacks, boys,
Built for the blacks, boys,
At the back is the Back of the Moon!

Back of the Moon, boys,
Back of the Moon, boys,
No one carries passes to the Back of the Moon.
By day you are boys, boys,
Now make a noise, boys,
Be a man at the Back of the Moon!

From the musical, King Kong[14]

*Shebeen: Illegal black bar/night club

And the townships generate many, many explanations and ideologies.

They do not always generate harmony.

Letters to the editor:

SIR,

I say No. I say that the hand that rocks the cradle is NOT the hand which should rule the world.

If one thinks deeply, one realises that men are at the heart of all worthwhile activities. Women are only there to finish them off when the real work has been done.

A home starts off as a house. A man suffers and struggles to build up a house—only later does a woman step in and makes it into a home. A woman is dependent on a man.

You need only to look at what is happening in the world, and you will see it is the men who are important, not women.

DANIEL KULA
Carletonville
Weekend World, April 10, 1977

SIR,

It's a good thing for Daniel Kula that he lives in Carletonville and not anywhere near me—as if I got hold of him I would make him sorry.

I would show him what a woman could do. I would put my big, strong, woman's arms around his scrawny, chicken-like male neck and he would soon change his ideas about the uselessness of women.

People like that make me sick. Especially the ones from South Africa. They are always wailing and complaining about how Blacks must be liberated from White oppression. But when it comes to the question of women they are traditionalists. They want women only for sex and cooking and washing, to put them to bed when they are drunk.

Women also have brains, and they also deserve liberation—not only from White rule, but from their own stupid men.

There are some good men, but most men are lazy drunken wasters.

If our Black men want to receive liberation, they should also be prepared to give liberation to their women.

Sir, please do not print my real name and address. I do not want my husband to see this letter. Please sign me with this name:

"MAMA"
Swaziland
Weekend World, April 17, 1977

Underneath the music, the myths, the language and even the disagreements, runs an awareness of the oppression of apartheid. The South African government robs Africans of their freedom of movement, the wealth their labor creates and the basic rights of family life. If you are not a vegetable or a willing slave, you must fight back.

Repression

Black South Africa has developed an urbanized culture, a culture of resistance. For the government this is a threat. In words, the government tries to ignore it or discredit it. In action, the government has tried to destroy it at its roots in the urban African communities.

The white authorities have always attempted to keep the African people from settling in cities. The Native Land Act of 1913 defined the limits of "native reserves." In 1923, the Urban Areas Act set controls on the flow of Africans into the towns. But only after the upsurge in strikes and labor militancy and the parallel rise of African political movements in the 1940s and '50s did the government develop a comprehensive program of social control.

The mainstay of this program is the concept of tribal "homelands" or Bantustans. The government claims that every African in South Africa originated in a tribe, each of which came from an officially designated "homeland." These homelands occupy less than 13 per cent of the total land area—whites own the other 87 per cent. The homelands are the most desolate, least-developed stretches of country. A family either slowly starves there, or the breadwinner applies to the authorities for a job in the "white" areas, alone. Far from encouraging an independent culture, the homelands barely let people survive.

In concert with the construction of the homelands in 1955, the government moved to "rationalize" the black urban population. "Unnecessary" people were shipped out to the homelands. The government created the vast modern townships, Soweto near Johannesburg and Mamelodi near Pretoria. They systematically destroyed "unauthorized" (i.e. well-established) black city districts such as Sophiatown. Africans whose families had owned houses in Johannesburg for generations saw them demolished, to be replaced by official four-room concrete boxes.

At this point, also, the government introduced the "dompass" (stupid-pass), as blacks named the passbook. Before, there were many separate pieces of paper—a residential pass, a work permit, and so on. Now, it all fits into one book, based on information kept in Pretoria's centralized computers.

And finally, the government introduced "Bantu Education."

> I just want to remind honourable members that if the native in South Africa today in any kind of school in existence is being taught to expect that he will live his adult life under a policy of equal rights, he is making a big mistake.
> *Verwoerd, then Minister of Native Affairs, introducing the Bantu Education Bill in 1953.*[15]

Education has never been equal for blacks and whites in South Africa. But when the Bantu Education Act came into operation in 1955, a policy of discrimination became a policy of repression. Africans were to be taught their place.

> When I have control of native education I will reform it so that natives will be taught from childhood to realize that equality with Europeans is not for them.
> *Verwoerd, introducing the Bantu Education Bill in 1953.*[16]

White students have free, compulsory education, blacks do not. The government spends $740 a year on each white child, and $48 on each black child. On average, a white classroom has 20 students to a teacher; a black classroom has 55 or more. Black teachers are mostly far less qualified—only one in ten would be accepted by a white school. Black students must pay for textbooks while whites receive them free. Black primary schools sometimes don't even have desks—the children sit on the floor.

Side by side with this crippling physical situation runs a crippling curriculum. In primary schools, African students must learn in their "own" African language, even in maths and sciences where they have to invent pseudo-African words for technical terms. In social studies, the student is only taught local events and places, learning little if any world history or geography.[17]

> What is the use of teaching a Bantu child mathematics when it cannot use it in practice? ... Education must train and teach people in accordance with their opportunities in life.
>
> *Verwoerd, to Senate, June 1954*

In secondary schools, African students were taught in English. In 1976, however, it was announced that in the future secondary students would be taught only in Afrikaans, the Dutch-derived language of the ruling white party. The students struck and demonstrated in protest against the new policy, which would limit their access to better jobs and the outside world, and force them to study a language traditionally associated with racism. From June 1976 to the present, the students have refused to return to "normal" studies under Bantu Education.

This concerted program—the homelands, the government townships, Bantu education, the dompass—became law in the mid-1950s. Over the past twenty years, the government has tightened and reinforced all these measures. It now intends to make the homelands "independent." In the case of the Transkei, it has done so. The homelands would still send their workers to earn a living in the "white" cities. But these workers would officially be aliens, foreigners with no claim to political rights or economic benefits from the Republic of South Africa.

To be sent to the "homeland" is a threat the government holds over every African urban resident. Shanty towns that become eyesores are bulldozed and the families who live in them are sent to the homelands, which many have never seen. During the 1976 riots, police raided the townships for pass offenders and "endorsed out" thousands of people. Teachers who complain of educational levels are told they can be reallocated to homeland schools. The goverment has given all African lawyers in Natal Province one year, until September 1978, to move out of the cities to the homelands. Between 1960 and 1970 the government uprooted and resettled more than three million black South Africans.[18]

In practice, how does the homelands policy function?

Jobs are hard to find in the homelands. So people have to find work in other places. There are more jobs in the towns. When your child starts working, he may want to work in town.

In South Africa the government controls the movement of people from the country to the town. So your child will not be allowed to go to town and look for a job. If he finds work in the town illegally, he may be arrested. This happens because his Reference Book is not stamped to show he has a job in town.

To get a stamp to work in town, your child must go to the Labour Officer in the homeland. Every homeland has a Labour Officer. The Labour Officer knows about jobs in town.

But your child will not be able to choose where he wants to work. The Labour Officer will tell him where he can work. Your child will not be allowed to move to town permanently. He can only go there to work for a short time. No person from the Homeland can get a house in the towns. So the whole family will not be allowed to move to town. Families of people working in the towns must stay in the country.

The job your child gets will last for about one year. Then he must go back to the Homeland. If he wants another job, he must go back to the Labour Officer. He must get another stamp to work.

If your child wants to work in town, he must first get a work seekers stamp. Go with your child to the nearest Labour Officer. Tell him you want your child to register as a work seeker. The Labour Officer will have a list of the kinds of work that are available. Ask him to read you this list. The choice your child makes is important. Your child will not be able to change from one kind of job to another. For example, if he chooses to be a domestic worker, he will have to go on working as a domestic worker.

Your child will be registered as a work seeker. But he still cannot go to town to look for work. He must wait until he is offered a job. A work seekers permit is not permission to go and look for work.

When your child is offered a job he will be told where it is. He will also be told how much money he will get. If he accepts the job he will have to sign a contract...

When your child gets to town his new employer must take him to the Labour Officer in the town. The Labour Officer will register him in the job. Your child's Reference Book will be stamped. This stamp will last for the time of the job. If your child stays in town after this time he may be arrested.

When the time of the contract is over, your child must leave his job. He must return to the Homeland where you live. The Law says he cannot look for another job in the town himself...

Many people from the country work in towns without a stamp. They are not legally registered to do their jobs. Many of these people are arrested every year. They spend time in prison. Then the government sends them back to their homes.

"Child Care," Lesson Ten, Weekend World, People's College, May 8, 1977

The homelands are a dead end.

Sunday Times, January 16, 1977

Whatever was traditional in the homelands has been eaten away. There is too little land or cattle for traditional agriculture, and even less capital for introducing more modern methods. The young and healthy leave, and send home their savings if they can. The homelands become the pensioners of the industrialized areas.

And there was a less glamourous side to all this. Wherever you went—in the fields, at village festivals, at church and every other place where people congregated—you found mostly middle-aged women, old women and old men. The land was not given out much. The Black man could only work the strip given him by the chief. The chief had no more land to give out. The old men at the fire-place complained endlessly that most of their lands had been taken away by the white man.

Ezekiel Mphahlele, Down Second Avenue, p. 23

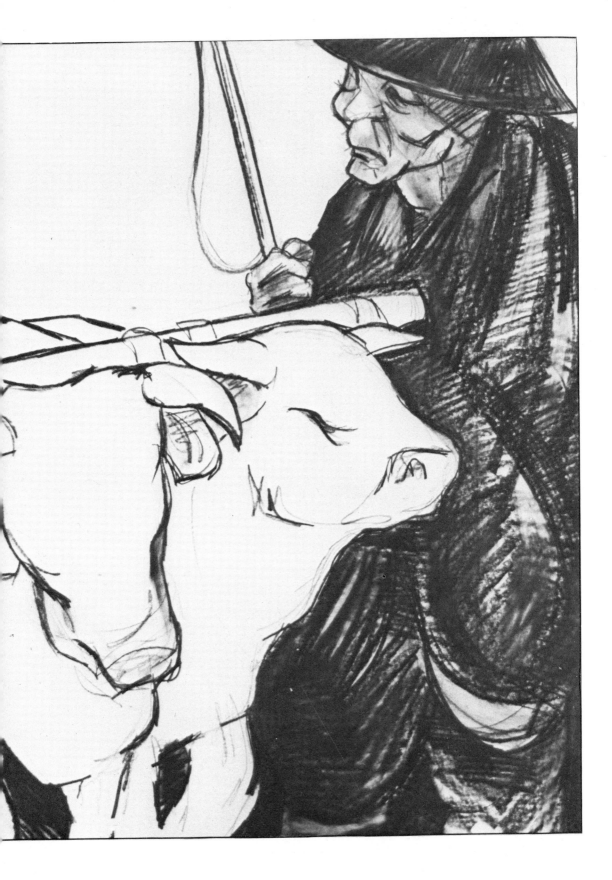

Erosion

A thirsty earth
Ribbed by rain it cannot catch
Overworked
Exhausted.

Tossing up its twisted green—
The joys from which we snatch
Our life.

J.S.

Even if the homelands were larger, they would still be unjustifiable. African workers made the bricks to build South Africa's cities. African fieldhands grew the white-owned crops of fruit, sugar and maize. African miners dug out the gold, diamonds, coal and uranium. Now these same Africans are told to return almost empty-handed to stagnant "tribal" areas, without any of the fruits of the industrialized economy to which they have given their working lives.

The pattern of migrant labor first grew up around the mines. By the late 1800s and early 1900s, when the mines were first developed, men came to work in them for a few months and then returned home to their villages. This was encouraged—the companies did not then have to support the miners' families. Men were housed in walled-in compounds, sleeping on concrete bunks, eating in communal halls. Miners did not become urbanized; their family roots remained in the countryside.

This is the "ideal state" to which South Africa's government would return. Africans would remain "ignorant country boys," accepting wages and working conditions that only "country boys" would accept. In 1976, black miners earned $104 a month; white miners over $690.[19]

> There is always a tension when mining is discussed; people's lives are deeply bound up in them, they are constant sources of employment, but the work is dangerous. Until recently the wages were far lower than for any other work (except perhaps for farm labour). The most generous remark made about the mines was "I hear they are paying better now." Ex-miners, mothers and wives alike were all outspoken in their condemnation of the mines: "I was earning R12 per month with free board and lodging. I saved R20.00 on my last contract of 10 months." (51-year-old mine worker.) "The mines do not care about their workers or about the Transkei." (62-year-old worker.) Some of the most bitter were those who were too old to work, had not benefitted from any of the wage increases in the early 1970s, and received no form of pension.
>
> *Transkei, p. 29*

The mines hunt far afield for migrant labor, in Mozambique, Angola, Malawi, Southern Rhodesia, Botswana, Lesotho and Swaziland. South African blacks avoid the mines if they can. Today 600,000 Africans work in the mines, about half from outside the Republic of South Africa. But with the rise of liberation movements to the north, the mining companies are relying more heavily upon the South African homelands to supply their workers.

The Bantustans have long fed the mines with labour, and indeed the Chamber of Mines was instrumental in pushing the 1913 Land Acts through Parliament—Acts which set borders to the "Reserves" and prohibited blacks from acquiring land on the open market. The Chamber of Mines, moreover, was closely involved with establishing the migrant system and the single-sex compound system. Today the Mining Houses are still major beneficiaries of the Bantustan system. Most migrants have spent at least a few years working on the mines. 473 of the [2066] men included in the survey had at one time or another worked on the mines; while 57 of the 654 away at the time of the survey were working on the mines. It is no wonder then that "the mines" play a part in the consciousness of people in the Transkei.

Transkei, p. 29

The men go to the cities and mines to work. The women are left to make do as best they can.

A survey of the Nqutu district of KwaZulu showed the average income of families of up to seven was R14,87 a month from migrant worker breadwinners.

This would buy two bags of mealie meal a month, at R7,20, leaving 47 cents over for other foods and clothes.

Sunday Tribune, June 27, 1976

The homelands have a more sinister side. On the one hand, they are a labor pool for industry; on the other, they are a rubbish heap for the people industry has no use for—the old, the sick, the very young. By law, if you cannot work you must go to your homeland, and there you are dumped. Sometimes there are "resettlement camps" of tents or huts for groups who are moved to a countryside that they do not know. Sometimes people are just left on the land, and told to survive off relatives. Schools are bad or non-existent, medical facilities the same. Some people survive. Many die. The homelands policy is a policy of polite extermination. Gas chambers are not needed when people can simply starve to death.

When people are too old or too ill to qualify as a "productive unit" they are endorsed out.

Once they are no longer able to sell their labour and are a burden to their community they are—according to the Bantu Urban Areas Act—required to be sent to their respective homelands...

Many of the people sent to the homelands were born in the cities and have no strong family ties in the homelands. There are no facilities to care for them and they are not wanted.

Weekend World, April 24, 1977

"I cannot mention my diet.
I think I eat only once in
three or four days."

> —*Widow, her only son last seen*
> *10 years ago.*
>
> *Transkei, p. 15*

LIFE is not a bed of roses for the Machabestad folks who were resettled on the late Chief Kebalepile Montshiwa's private farm about 11 kilometres from Mefeking in 1971.

Last week I went out to investigate the living conditions of these people. They were dumped in this place in 1971, and were told they would remain on it for only three months before being given land equivalent to what they had previously owned in Machabestad. "But nix. We are still here," they said.

These people claim that Machabestad—a few kilometres from Potchefstroom—was their land for many years. "We had a title deed for it," they said.

They now still live in shacks despite the fact that it is seven years since they have moved to the Mafeking area.

WORN OUT

The tents that were put up when they were first brought to the farm are worn out. Most of the shacks are rusted and many families have put up mud houses which dissolve each time it rains. "Because of living conditions in this area we have had more deaths than ever before," they said.

World, April 19, 1977

Nqusi Household No. 8—Income: 0 (All income figures in Rand per year.*)

This family comprises 5 people: husband and wife of 65 and 60 years old; husband's mother of 80 years old; their daughter of 24 and her daughter of 13 years old. They live in two rondavaals, thatched, and built of mud bricks. They have no windows, but ventilation holes set in the walls.

The sole furnishings are 3 grass mats, a mud sitting bench has been built into the wall. They own stock: 2 cattle, 5 sheep, 6 goats and 4 fowls. They also have a dog.

They are allotted a field but are unable to use it because they have no means of ploughing. They cultivate only a small garden of mealies and vegetables. They have no income. None of the old people has managed to get a pension. They are assisted by other residents as far as food and clothing are concerned. Their son has left to work but has not yet sent anything home.

Their diet is samp, mealies and vegetables. Twice a year they eat meat.

Transkei, p. 20

---

*Out of 757 families in the Transkei surveyed, 50 families, or 233 people, had no income whatsoever. The study comments, "All the [destitute] families somehow manage to claw out a subsistence diet— those who fail to do so die."

The elderly die of starvation and neglect disguised as old age; the children die of starvation either outright as kwashiorkor (protein deficiencies) or under the disguise of gastro-enteritis or some other disease. The South African government does not publish figures for infant mortality in the African population, but studies have showed that in some areas a third to two-thirds of all children born die before they are three. More than one in 100 children in the black population as a whole "by a very conservative estimate" die of outright starvation. And it is getting worse. In Natal, the 1976 death toll of malnourished children was put at four times that of 1974, and three times that of 1975.[20]

Five babies are dying a day from gastro-enteritis at the Thornhill Camp, the Queenstown public health inspector, Mr W. Coetzee, has warned in a memorandum on the threat to 25 km from Queenstown.

The Chief Minister of the Ciskei, Mr Lennox Sebe, and members of the Ciskei Cabinet, yesterday made on-the-spot inspections at Thornhill, about 25 km from Queenstown.

According to Dr Barbara Seidler, who is in charge of the immunisation programme, the arrival of the Cabinet comes at a time when the death rate has mounted to five or more a day.

Nobody in this shanty town could give an exact count of deaths for December, or in January, so far, she said.

"The babies are dying of gastro-enteritis and diarrhoea," she said.

"The adult deaths are attributable to malnutrition and consequent incidence of diseases like kwashiorkor, tuberculosis and pellagra."

A Frontier Hospital spokesman estimates that Dr Seidler has inoculated every man, woman and child on Thornhill, about 30 000 people.

Yesterday she continued her 14-hour-a-day stint at her makeshift hospital in the bare, unfurnished rooms of the former Thornhill farmhouse.

The superintendent of the Frontier Hospital, Dr R. Schaeffer, said yesterday: "I am satisfied Dr Seidler has done absolutely excellent work in providing medical and sanitary facilities in the all-too-short time she has been given.

"I have no absolute knowledge of the Thornhill death toll, but it stands to reason this must be high among the undernourished, no matter where they are."

Rand Daily Mail extra, Jan. 10, 1977

The whites dine in Holiday Inns. They see "their" black domestic servants and workers as happy, singing natives. Why should anyone complain?

Liberation

> Do you seek possession of my country? I and my people are resolved that that you shall not have. We have no confidence in you, and you have neither love nor pity for us. We are Kaffirs, which means we are dogs or monkeys to be shot down or otherwise ill-treated as you may find it convenient. These are not mere idle words, but they are words of sorrow every day.
>
> *Letter from Khama III, King of the BamaNgwato,*
> *to Transvaal Boers, 11 March 1877*

The people of South Africa have never accepted white rule. It was imposed with guns and clubs, and each new measure has had to be backed up with new violence. The African kingdoms fought the advancing white settler frontier for centuries, war after war after war. The last rebellion was wiped out by machine-gun fire in 1906.

Also in 1906, the Transvaal introduced pass laws for the Indian population. In response, Mahatma Gandhi led the first passive resistance campaign, but had little success.

The Union of South Africa was formed in 1910. The African National Congress of South Africa, a black political party fighting for democratic political rights for blacks, was formed in 1912.

There have been strikes and black trade unions, successful and unsuccessful. In 1927 the ICU (Industrial and Commercial Workers Union of Africa) had a membership of 100,000. The ANC and the ICU together initiated an anti-pass movement: Mayibuye. The government confronted it with force: arrests, batons, guns.

MAYIBUYE I AFRIKA (May Africa Return)

Tina Sizwe esi ntsundu	We the people who are brown
Sikalel'i Afrika	Bless Africa
eyahlutw' obawo betu	which was taken from our fathers
besese bu' mnyameni.	when they were in darkness.
Mayibuye, mayibuye,	Let it return, let it return,
Mayibuy'i Afrika!	Let Africa return to us!
Makapele namapasi	Down with passes
Sitoli nkululeko.	We demand Freedom

written by N.B. Tantsi for the anti-pass campaign of 1928
Tune: Clementine[21]

The 1940s and '50s saw further protest. In 1946, 100,000 black miners struck: the authorities beat them back. In 1949, the ANC Youth League began the "Programme of Action." In June 1952, an ANC passive resistance campaign against the pass laws led to the arrest of over eight thousand demonstrators. Then riots broke out in East London, Port Elizabeth, Kimberley, on the Rand. Police opened fire. Parliament responded by passing laws carrying heavy penalties against anyone who broke a law in political protest.

In 1956, the government declared that women must carry passes as well as men. Women marched, burned their pass books. In 1956, 20,000 women demonstrated in Pretoria. Their slogan: "Strijdom [then-prime minister] you have struck a rock once you have struck a woman."[22]

In December 1956, the government arrested 156 leaders of the liberation movement and charged them with attempting to overthrow the government by force. The trials continued for four years.

In 1959, the ANC, since the 1940s the only black political force, split and a splinter group was formed. It was called the Pan Africanist Congress.

In 1960, police opened fire on a peaceful demonstration against the pass laws in Sharpeville. Sixty-two people died. The government declared a state of emergency; the ANC and PAC were banned. Both decided to oppose government violence with armed resistance.

Their leaders were arrested, convicted, sentenced to life imprisonment. Among them: Nelson Mandela. Govan Mbeki. Walter Sisulu. They remain in Robben Island maximum security prison today—life imprisonment for political prisoners in South Africa means just that. The lawyer who defended them, an Afrikaner from a prominent family, was arrested and sentenced to life imprisonment. (Bram Fischer completed his sentence. He died of cancer in 1975.)

For the moment, the ANC and PAC seemed effectively silenced. Industry boomed. Government debated whether it should remove the "whites only" signs from park benches. Liberal critics recovered from the shocks of Sharpeville, the sabotage, the trials. Apartheid appeared to have stabilized. Any disturbances could be attributed to malcontents living abroad.

Then, in June 1976, a simmering student protest against Bantu Education in Soweto exploded after the police opened fire on a crowd. Township residents across South Africa fought back with stones, bottles or arson, attacking the Bantu Administration Boards, the government liquor stores, the bus companies, the police and police informers. The apparent quiescence was shattered.

Abantu bakithi bahluphekile
Vukani Madoda
Silwele ilizwe lethu
Ela thathwa

Siqale ngo Smith
Sigcine ngo Vorster
Baphele Bonke
Vukani Madoda!
Silwele ilizwe lethu
Ela thathwa

Our people are suffering
Wake up men!
Let us fight for our country
Which they took.

We shall start with Smith
And end with Vorster
And destroy them all
Wake up men!
Let us fight for our country
Which they took.

Southern African folksong

Soweto now means more than a government township: it has become a symbol of resistance.

Soweto

A playground
Where hippos bark
And nylons rip into the crowd
And children die
For hope to be born.

J.S.

Slang: *Hippo*—an armored truck which carries riot police;
nylons—Black Marias so full of arrested people that
they burst at the seams

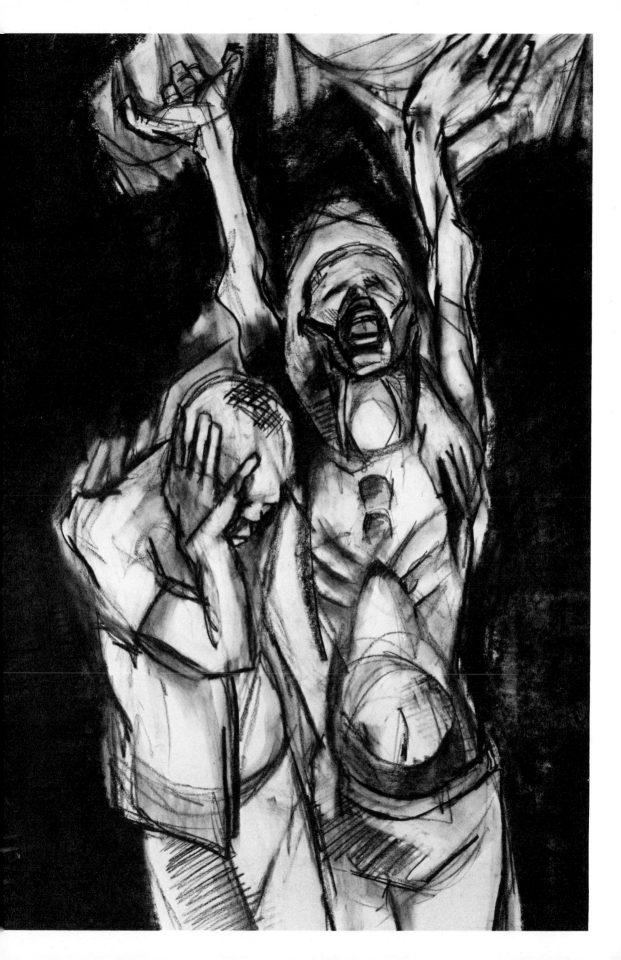

No one knows the final count of the dead from the 1976 riots. The Rand Daily Mail compiled a list of 499 names from funeral parlor, police and hospital records; later they revised it to include well over 600 names. There are

unsubstantiated rumors of mass graves filled at night. But even without these, many people believe the figure is much higher, probably closer to a thousand killed.

E

Edelstein, Melville Leonard, Eesterhuizen, Johannes Hendrik.

F

Follie, Enoch (June 18), shot above the heart.

G

•Gincana, Atwell (June 18), •Godwe Jeffrey (June 18).

K

•Kalane, George; •Kekane, Shadrack; •Keokame, Marshall (June 16); •Kgampe, Philemon; •Kgapule, Edward, •Kgongoana, Ariel "Pro" (June 16); •Kgupisi, Herbert; •Khumalo, Daniel (June 19); •Kobedi, Kabelo (June 25); •Kubeka, Johannes, 24, (June 17), gunshot wounds of left leg, died of haemorrhage;. •Kubheka, Robert; •Kumalo, Zolile (June 17); •Kumalo, Nehemia; •Kunene, Norman, 27, (June 17); •Kwinana, Gregory, (June 17)

L

•Ledwaba, Jacob; •Lepota David; •Leroke, Hermina; •Linda, Petrus King, killed by bullet; •Lengwathi, Patrick Themba (June 12), shot; •Lloyd, Jan, 26; •Luvatsha, Thembo, bullet wounds below stomach.

M

•Mabaso, Mathabeni; •Mabuku, Gladys; •Madzivhandila Patrick; •Magadani, Florence; •Mahasha, Daniel; •Mahlambi, Paulina; •Mahlanza, Raymond; 24, (June 17), shot in hip; •Mahapo, Godfrev; •Maipa, Simon; •Majola, Boy; •Makhari, Abraham, 33; •Makhabane, Petrus K, shot in stomach and chest; hotla, •Manganyi, Victor; •March, Phillip (June 20), shot thrice through head and stomach; •Masenya, Grace; •Masinga, David, 19, (June 16); •Mathebula, Jacob Sydney. •Mathebula, Josiah; •Matome, Mackenzie; •Matsapola, E., two bullet wounds; •Matsepe, Jeffrey; •Matsunyane, James Sello, shot at the back — bullet went through the body. •Mavimbela, Sipho; •Manale, Herbert; •Mbebe, Frank; •Mchunu Moses; •Mda, John, 32, (June 17), gunshot wounds of chest and lung; •Menwe, Peter; •Mevana, David, shot through sternum; •Mhlanga, Samuel. •Mhlongo, Felix (June 18), shot — wound involving lung, heart and spinal column; •Mithi, Lily; •Mkhize, Tusokwakhe; •Mkhotlana, Elias, 43; •Mkhwanazi, Israel; •Mkhwanazi, Lindiwe; • Mlangeni, Lea; •Mmutle, D., bullet through the side; •Mnculwane, Mantombi P., shot; •Mngemane, Morris, five bullet wounds. •Mngoma, Tenson; •Mngomezulu, Simon, 29, (June 18); •Mphetha, Lawrence. •Modukanele, Jacob; •Modukanele, Isaac Rasebata; •Moerane, Jacob, 23 (June 19), burnt under vehicle; •Mogola, Johannes; •Mokgatle, Moses; •Mogapi, Stephen; •Mokoena. Moses; •Mokoena, Vincent; •Moleko, Hendrick, (June 18), shot in the stomach. •Montjane, Elijah; •Mononyane, Joseph S. (June 18); •Msimanga, Mbekiseni; •Mthembo, John; •Mtshadi, Simon; •Mubuya, Ben-

P

•Phakathi, Charles; Peterson, Hector, 13, (June 16); among the first riot victims to die; •Patrick, Petrus; •Pindela, Nelson.

R

•Radebe, Mpikeleli Jeremiah; •Radebe, Susie; •Raditlhalo, Alfred; •Rambuda, Bethuel; •Ruiters, Harry.

S

•Sealetsa, Samuel Ntsamo. •Segegede, Jan; Selane, Charles; Senatle, Vincent; •Shabangu, Doctor. •Sihlangu, Elizabeth; •Simelane, Benjamin; . •Sithole Benjamin; •Sithole, Douglas; •Sithole, Samuel.

T

•Taaka, Louis, bullet wound on groin; •Taunyana, David; •Tefu, Madimetja Lucas; •Teisi, Gabriel; •Thobejane, Ida; •Tokota, Kenny; •Tshabalala, Christopher; •Tshabalala, Godfrey; •Tshabalala, Titus; •Tshabalala, Michael; •Tshabalala, Sarah; •Tshabalala, Veronica. •Twala, Thomas, 21; •Tyiki, Robert, 15, (June 17), gunshot wounds of heart.

People listed as "unknown" by the Johannesburg inquest court and only identified by the following "serial" numbers: 1528; 1529; 1530; 1531; 1532; 1533; 1534; 1535; 1536; 1537; 1538; 1539; 1540; 1541; 1542; 1543; 1544; 1545; 1546; 1547; 1548; 1549; 1551; 1553; 1555; 1559; 1560; 1629; 1630; 1631; 1632; 1633; 1634; 1635; 1941; 1997; 1998.

V

•Vilankulu, Mangoeng Joseph, shot; •Van Rooyen, Aubrey Vincent.

W

•Wilson, Margaret, shot.

Y

•Yiba, Monde.

Z

•Zondo, Simon Gosson, 18, (June 18), gunshot wounds; •Zungu, Phillip; •Wandile, John, burn wound in abdomen.

THE list of dead obtained from a Soweto undertaker. Causes of death contained in post mortem reports:

Titus Tshwene, 13 died Aug 27 of multiple shotgun pellet wounds of lungs.

Johannes Sibeko, 48, died Sept 7 gunshot wounds of chest and abdomen.

Makhosi Makhotla, 46, died Sept 7 gunshot wounds of abdomen.

Joyce Buthelezi, 16, died Sept 17 shotgun wounds of chest and head.

Sylvester Vusi Maseko, 21, Sept 20 gunshot wounds of the head.

Lawrence Mshelwane, 27, gunshot wounds of abdomen.

Gunstan Kwadi, 32, Aug 26 gunshot wounds of head.

Raymond Mofokeng, 14, Aug 25 gunshot wounds of chest and neck.

Petrus Gule, 15, Aug 26 gunshot wounds of head.

Washington Makate, 26, Aug 25 shotgun pellet wounds of both legs, died of haemorrhage.

Patrick Nkosi, 20, Aug 27 bullet wound through neck with contusion of medulla oblongata.

Sara Maseko, 46, June 17 gunshot wounds of thighs died of haemorrhage.

Samson Fantu Kalakahla, 26,

J

Jacobs, Mervyn. 38 Street Elsies River. Sept 8. Shot.

Jacobs, Shaheed, 15. years. District Six. Died Sept 6. Shot.

K

Kamese, Adries. 28 years. NY 156 No 17, Guguletu. Aug 12. Shot dead.

Kamfer, Benjamin. 16 years. 39, 11th Avenue, Ravensmead. Sept 10. Shot dead.

Khan, Naziem. 15 years. Mannenberg. Sept 16.

Kleinsmith, Angelaire, 29 years, 14th Avenue, Elsie's River. Sept 8.

Khumalo, Joseph. Guguletu. Sept 10.

L

Lee, Ralph. 16 years. Retreat Road, Retreat. Died Sept 8. Shot

Limba, B. Guguletu. Sept 16. 19.

Lucas, Cornelius. Mossel Bay. Died prior to Sept 15.

Lutya, Wiseman. 23 years. Guguletu. Aug 12.

M

Man: Youth shot dead in Guguletu. Unidentified. Police. opened fire on "mob" approaching police station. (Cape Times 26 October, 1976.)

Man: Shot dead by Police — allegedly throwing petrol bomb. Unidentified. (Cape Times 13 Oct 76.)

Marnie, Alfred. 18. Retreat. Shot Sept 9.

McAnthony Siziba, 11, Aug 26.
Jonathan Siziba, 5, Aug 26.
Eric Mabaso, 18.
Gordon Nkuta, 19, July 25.
Titus Moatse, 15, July 19.
Joyce Hlatshwayo, 4.
Jacob Phiri, 28, June 28.
Jacob Twala, 18, Oct 30.
Samuel Tsotetsi, 18, Nov 1.

Another list from a Soweto undertaker accompanied by official death certificates.

Johannes Hlongwane, 43, Sept 12.
Petros Hlongwane, 29, July 25.
Zabulon Kubheka, 47, Aug 22.
Hilton Kubheka, 19, July 16.
Peter Letsholo, 21, Aug 25.
Inspector Luphindo, 24, July 2.
John Leburu, 23, June 18.
Mbopha Mthembu, 18, Sept 14.
Johan Mathobela, 19, Aug 12.
Reuben Mthembu, 19, Aug 2.
George Malindisa, 23, July 31.
Titus Majola, 15, July 19.
John Molefe, 19, June 25.
Monica Nkosi, 6, Aug 1.
Jacob Moerane, 23, June 19 burnt under vehicle.
Norurau Nkonyane, 34, Aug 10.
Timothy Ndlovu, 36, June 18.
Jeffrey Tshabalala, 24, July 17.
Johannes Mashaba 22, strangulation
Lesley Hastings Ndlovu, 17, June 16 of 7235 Orlando West.

David Mahlaba, 24.
Hector Ndlela, 20.
Vivian Thabethe, 27.
Peter Molefe, 21.
Oben Ngcobo, 17.
Walter Maichetha, 15.

Cases investigated Sunday Times Extra reporter.

Dumisani Isaac Mbatha, 16, Sept 25 at Far East Rand Hospital, detained during central Johannesburg unrest.

Maxwell Mahlinza, 24, June 17 shot in the hip.

Ndingane, M. 13 yea Guguletu. Died Sept 15. Shot.

Nduna, Kenneth. 38 years. 4 tenheut Street, Langa. August 1976. Shot dead.

Nezumga, Nicholas Silo years. NY 140, No 7, Gugu August 11. Shot dead.

Ngxgabi, Joseph. 22 ye Guguletu. August 12.

Nixxey, Basil. 42 years. N nenberg, Sept 9.

Nonkasa, Victor. NY 10, Nc Guguletu. Sept 19, 1976. Shot d Nteko, Telford Muuseledo. years. Guguletu. August 12.

October, Ronald. 18 yea Welcome Estate. Died Sept 16.

Olifant, Harrison. 15 years. 12, Room 64, Guguletu. October Shot dead.

Opperman, Michael John. years. Died Sept 9 of guns wounds received at Hanover Pa

P

Paulsen. 14A Kaseyaweg, M nenberg. Sept 9. Shot dead.

Peters, Sandra. 11 years years), Athlone. Died Sept 4. S

Peters, Phyllis. 43 yea Athlone. Sept 16.

Petersen, G. J. 22 years. Avenue, Retreat. Died Sept 8. S

S

Sogiba, Bettfund. 11 years. Nyanga East. Letter in Cape T

while detained at Johannesb Fort.

Sinki Witboy, 6, died in pet bomb attack in parents' house Zola.

Aaron Mbele, struck by bulle Sipho Clement Mbatha, 22.

Robert Tseke, 19, shot throu the head on Aug 6.

Agnes Moatlhudi, 10 of 168 Zc 1, Meadowlands.

Thomas Sibanyoni, 10.

Seuntjie Sibanyoni, 5.

List obtained from a Mof North undertaker, containi names of people who died dur the Soweto unrest:

Timothy Nhlapo, 31, of Dlamini No 1.

Vusimuzi Ngubane, 34, of Zondi 2.

Jeremiah Rasmen, 18, of 8 Zola 3.

Jumba Gumata, 26, of 2 Rockville.

Godfrey Khambule, 12, of Mofolo North.

Stanley Mbengwane, 28, of Zola North.

Simon Mbele, 19, of 1474 Zond John Radebe, 35, of 2092 b Zol.

The Black Parents' Associati a body formed in Soweto soon a the unrest, committed itself provide funeral and relief tions which totalled R47 082, 60 183 people who either lost th lives or were injured during disturbances.

There were 107 victims burie Soweto through the help of BPA. Among them were:

Reginald Luvatsha of 1800 P ville.

Boas Sydney Masilo of 873a Zc Mnyane Jacob Nkofu of 2 Pimville.

Samuel Shihlomule of Central Western Jabavu.

Abel Jan Matsabu of 106 Orlando West.

Gustov Kgoadi of 4

From a list compiled by E. Duma of riot dead, December 31, 1976

While the shooting continued, the anti-treason and sabotage laws of South Africa came into play. The government can detain anyone without giving the cause, until such time as it decides to release them. It uses these powers without hesitation. There were at least 5,200 people arrested, charged or detained without trial in the first three months of the 1976 riots.[23] Of those brought to trial by December, 1381 people were convicted.[24] Detainees are not tried.

The government also has the "banning order." A person who has been banned becomes a non-person: he or she cannot talk to more than two people at a time, cannot leave a restricted area or be published or quoted. Banned people remain under strict police surveillance. Although this almost always means giving up a job, the government rarely provides compensation. A banning order does not cease when a person dies: their words still may not be quoted or published. A banning order effectively eliminates any potential community leader. Again, no reason need be given.

Some of the people jailed under the treason laws have been let out; some are still in detention. More are arrested every week, from all sections of society. Now, the police especially arrest students, since the riots were led by schoolchildren.

People disappear—whether they fled South Africa or were arrested, or died, their families do not know. At one point there were reported to be 5000 children missing from Soweto alone.[25]

In fact, from the lawyer's point of view, it is impossible in South Africa today to distinguish between times of normality and emergency...

Let me be more specific. The emergency regulations issued in 1960 covered a number of different subjects: the control and dispersal of gatherings; preventive statements; the suppression of subversive associations; and detention for interrogation...

●**Preventive Detention:**

Regulation Four of the emergency regulations empowered the Minister of Justice, a magistrate and any commissioned officer in the Defence or Police Force to detain any person indefinitely where he was of the opinion that such detention was "desirable in the interests of public order or safety, or of that person, or for the termination of a state of emergency."

Magistrates could in similar circumstances and with the authority of the Minister, "control" the activities of any person.

Similar powers have now been conferred on the Minister of Justice in terms of Sections Nine and 10 of the Internal Security Act.

In general terms, the Minister can employ these powers "if he is satisfied that any person engages in activities which...endanger, or are calculated to endanger, the security of the State or the maintenance of public order..."

The powers of restriction (house arrest) are permanently available. The preventive detention provisions can only be used if brought into operation by the State President. This has been done in the case of the present riots and the powers have been used extensively.

●**Detention for Interrogation:**

Regulation 19 of the emergency regulations empowered the Minister of Justice, the Commissioner of Police, any commissioned officer in the Defence or Police Force and any magistrate, to arrest and detain any person for interrogation if satisfied, or in certain cases, he had reason to suspect, that the person intended to commit, or had information relating to "any offence... committed with the intention to hamper the maintenance of public order or to endanger the safety of the public..."

The preventive detention provisions under the Internal Security Act could undoubtedly be used for this purpose. In addition, however, since 1962 Parliament has enacted no fewer than five provisions which authorise detention for interrogation for a variety of offences...

Perhaps the most formidable of these provisions is Section Six of the Terrorism Act of 1967.

This empowers a police officer of or above the rank of lieutenant-colonel, to detain a person "if he has reason to believe that person...is a terrorist or is withholding...any information relating to terrorists" or terrorism.

"Terrorism" includes hampering or deterring "any person from assisting in the maintenance of law and order." The detention lasts until either the Commissioner of Police is satisfied that the detainee has "satisfactorily replied to all questions" put to him, or "that no useful purpose will be served by his further detention," or the Minister orders his release.

The conditions of detention are determined by the Commissioner of Police "subject to the directions of the Minister", but no person can have access to the detainee other than the Minister and officers in the service of the State.

Prof. W.B. Dean, University of Cape Town, in Rand Daily Mail extra, Nov. 16, 1976

After arrest, there is torture, beatings, and electric shock. Almost every week now another person dies while in the custody of the police.

> I am convinced that nobody detained by our police is safe. There have been many, many deaths in detention, and we as black people are convinced now that for a black man to enter a gaol is almost like entering a grave.
> *Gatsha Buthelezi, on the death of Steve Biko in detention*
> *Rand Daily Mail extra, Sept. 14, 1977*

GOD is great. The words of the Ranoto children who have now learnt to live without their parents, who were detained in January.

Mr and Mrs Marcus Ranoto were detained under Section Six of the Terrorism Act. The children have not seen them since.

The children, Rebecca (19), Abie (14), Nkele (12) and Sina (10) are living as "orphans" in their Tladi home in Soweto. "We are living on charity although our parents are alive, somewhere in a jail," said the eldest of the children, Rebecca.

When a team of WORLD reporters arrived at the Ranoto home last night, the children were being visited by two of their relatives. Two of the children, Sinah and Nkele were not at home. They had been sent to a house nearby.

Despite the fact that their parents are both in detention, they looked happy. It was clear that relatives, family friends and charitable organisations are doing a good job of looking after the children.

COOKING

A number of new school books were packed on the sideboard in the dining room.

Shortly after our arrival, Rebecca, a Form Four student at Sekano Ntoane High School, lit up the house. She had been cooking for her younger sisters and brother.

She jokingly said: "I am a mother in this house. But I can't get used to the fact that our parents are in jail. That

JUST when will the end come? These were the words of a Soweto mother who this week told of how she spends sleepless nights worrying over her five children she has never seen since the beginning of the year.

Mrs Khosi Mbatha's anguish started on January 31, when her 44-year-old husband, Mr Alexandra Mbatha, was detained by security police at their Dube home.

Her two elder daughters, Chalotte (17) and Nomsa (19) disappeared and have never been seen again.

Her other three children, Linda (14), Sibuxixo (10) and Zanele

(6) are destitute in Swaziland where they have been attending school.

Her husband has now been released after spending more than three months in solitary confinement under Section Six of the Terorrism Act. Mr Mbatha was not present when I arrived at his home. He has been a sick man since his release. He was taken to a doctor who advised that he receive treatment regularly.

The saddest thing about the Mbatha parents is that they do not know if their two elder daughters are being detained somewhere in a

MANY husbands a wives, mothers a fathers have be affected by the continu detention witho charges of members their families.

One such family is t of Joe Thloloe, WORLD journalist a president of the Union Black Journalists. He now been in detention 76 days—his seco stretch inside a year. he is only one of man

Many a Black man faced with problems it is worse if they blind. This is t situation of Mr Jo Mothopeng, a blind ma who has been stay with his younger brot since their parents we detained last year.

His father, Mr Ze Mothopeng was detain in August while mother Mrs Uban Mothopeng was detain on November 15 last ye under Section Six of t Terrorism Act and he h

THE disappearance of children as well as adults, folowed alleged police raids, has resulted in frantic searches at police stations and prisons by relatives and parents.

Soweto's new police chief, Brigadier J.F. Visser, told the Rand Daily Mail yesterday that those missing relatives should approach him at Protea police headquarters.

Mr M. Sithusha, principal of Phulong Secondary school in Kwa Thema, Springs, said yesterday he had been searching for four male teachers at his school who were picked up by police at their homes last Tuesday without success.

Brigadier J.B. Wiese, Divisional Commissioner of Police for the East Rand, said later in an interview that the four teachers were being detained in Springs, where they were still being questioned by the Security Police.

A Johannesburg domestic servant, Rephina

Beloi, has been spending sleepless nights trying to trace her two young daughters, who disappeared on Sunday.

The children, Naomi, 15, and Leslie, 13, both pupils at Mathsidiso Higher Primary School, left their home at 8778 A, Orlando West, on Sunday afternoon after saying they were going to play with others. They never returned, said their mother.

Her employer, who asked not to be identified, said she had phoned various police stations in search of the missing girls, but could not trace them.

One father said he was working in his garden at Tladi in Soweto on Saturday when he noticed children running by the gate. His daughter, aged 11, and his niece, eight, rushed to the gate to see what was happening.

He said two Black policemen, wearing camouflage uniforms, appeared and loaded his

MRS Mary Pitso, wife a West Rand Admin tration Board seni clerk, Mr Ambrose Pits yesterday told how h husband and son we arrested during a poli swoop in the early hou of Friday last week.

Mrs Pitso, of Sowe said that at about 2 a there was a knock at t door which her husba answered. "About sev White policemen enter and told my husband

From: World, May 11, 18; Rand Daily Mail, ext 18, 1977; Rand Daily M extra, Nov. 10 1976 and J 2, 1977

daughter and niece onto police truck. He said went to John Vors Square on Monday aft

The rulers stood on the sand
And demanded
That the tide turn back.

They even shot it.

Who shall blame the water
When they drown?

White South Africa is nervous. Those who can, consider leaving. Those who must stay, buy guns. Following the 1976 riots, gun sales (restricted to whites only) became phenomenal. At the University of Zululand, white staff members bought for their own use $17,250 worth of guns.[26] Newspapers report that one can no longer safely get into an argument at a traffic light—if the other guy is white he is likely to start shooting. Women's pages in white newspapers carry articles on a new design of bra made to carry a pistol while still maintaining sex appeal.

Apartheid wages a war against the black people of South Africa, using every weapon of repression—from starvation to torture to military annihilation. Is it any more of a war if the people fight back?

They are fighting back.

No one really knows the extent of the conflict today. We know that the riots are continuing, that people are being shot by the police, that schools and beerhalls are being burnt down. (Riots now appear on page 3, column 2; they barely count as news. Reports are cryptic and compressed.)

Hundreds of students are escaping across the borders, many to join guerrilla training camps in free Africa. How many are coming back?

DIARY OF A MONTH—AUGUST 1977
(from South African press reports)

Aug. 1—Police reinforcements patrol Soweto after weekend riots. Police chief announced new "get tough" policy. Police charge mourners at funeral of detainee who died in prison.

Aug. 2—Girl student dies. Police raid Seanamerena Jr. Secondary School.

Aug. 3—Youth shot by police in raid on Orlando East Secondary School. Police set dogs on students. Police patrolling township streets. A number of youths detained. Several schools stoned. Schools in Atteridgeville-Saulsville enter second week of boycott.

Aug. 4—One youth shot dead in Soweto, "Unrest spreads." Four children hit by buckshot. Continuous rioting, Mamelodi schools closed by students. Unrest in Ga Rankuwa. Kimberly bus boycott against increased fares enters fifth week.

Aug. 5—Police in Soweto arrest 82; six incidents and house raids, police fired and used dogs on crowd. No one reported dead. Institute of Race Relations reports 18 people have died in detention since March 1976; 579 people are believed to be in detention.

Aug. 6—Ban on public meetings extended for one year.

Aug. 7—Security police detain 7 Soweto Student Representative Council (SSRC) members. "Heavy police contingents" patrol Soweto; no rioting reported. Evidence that most black students who received a "pass" in last year's Junior Certificate exams, which had been boycotted, have actually failed.

Aug. 9—Evaton riots: 230 students arrested, post office van burnt. 12 arrested in Soweto, 3 injured.

Aug. 10—Cape Town: Modderdam shantytown bulldozed, 26,000 people left homeless. 22 students arrested in East Rand; 3 girls slightly injured; school boycotts in Atteridgeville become violent. The search for the Ga Rankuwa arsonists still continues—Barclays Bank in Ga Rankuwa gutted by fire.

Aug. 15—66 students arrested at funeral of girls shot 2 weeks ago. Students decide to end school boycott.

"Terrorist news" is now censored in South African newspapers, except for brief police releases.

Several terrorist bases, some close to Durban and others on the Reef, have been wiped out by heavily armed police and a number of terrorists have been captured.

Rand Daily Mail,
Aug 29, 1977

SOWETO police yesterday arrested 82 people...
Major General Kriel described yesterday as a "quiet day" compared to Tuesday...there were six incidents and no one was killed...

World, Aug. 5, 1977

Aug. 16—Police detain 11 more SSRC members. Police raid Klipspruit school, no violence.

Aug. 17—Police raid four secondary schools in Soweto, arrest 130 youths, 45 others arrested at Nancefield. At Orlando West secondary school, police fired birdshot, used dogs. SSRC continued back-to-school call.

Aug. 18—Police detain 36 in Soweto school raids. Minister of Bantu Education threatens to close all Soweto schools. Six schools raided; students chased out and beaten.

Aug. 20—One shot dead, 137 detained in Soweto. In Port Elizabeth, 22 crowd "ringleaders" detained.

Aug. 22—Black People's Convention meeting raided; 2 members of Committee of 10" (unofficial council of Soweto community leaders) and several BPC leaders detained.

Aug. 23—West Rand Administration Board admits the "Committee of 13," the government's answer to the Committee of 10, whom WRAB has repeatedly cited as their community support, is a joke and never existed. 13 students arrested at Molofo school; school attendence "low."

Aug. 25—University of the North (Turfloop) on strike. Pretoria school violence, one wounded in shooting.

Aug. 26—Government announces all Soweto schools are to be closed and reopened under direct control of the government (i.e. eliminating school boards). One shot dead in riot at Jabulani Junior Secondary School. Turfloop University closed.

Aug. 28—Burial of man who died in Ga Rankuwa explosion at Boekenhout-fontein High School.

Aug. 29—Minister of Justice threatens to close the "World" newspaper. Police claim to have captured arms caches, terrorist bases in Natal.

Aug. 30—All Soweto secondary and high school students told they must re-register at new State-run schools. Atteridgeville and Mamelodi schools boycotted. One Soweto school stoned.

Aug. 31—Boycott of schools in Atteridgeville, schools stoned. Riot in East London dispersed by dogs. Turfloop students told to reapply for admission to university.

Their struggle is a truly
national one. It is a struggle of
the African people, inspired by
their own suffering and their
own experience. It is a struggle
for the right live.

—Nelson Mandela, leader of
the African National Congress
now serving life imprisonment
on Robben Island.
(No Easy Walk to Freedom,
p. 189)

Abantu Ba ye Zwa

Abantu: (Zulu) the people
Zwa: (Zulu) hear; listen; taste; smell; feel; sense; live, be alive

The people live.

THE FUTURE IS OURS

FREE SOUTHAFRICA

Appendix A: Chronology

1820s-'30s   *Mfecane* and *difiqane* wars. Rise of Zulu under Shaka; Ndebele become Mzilikazi; Tlokwa under Queen MaNtatisi; Sotho under Moshoeshoe, etc.

1830s-'40s   Boer invasion of the interior (present Transvaal, Orange Free State, Natal).

1870s   Diamond mines opened around Kimberley

1870s-'80s   British and German scramble for the interior. African wars of resistance—Pedi under Sekukhuni, Zulu under Cetewayo, etc.

1880s-'90s   Gold mining on the Witwatersrand (around Johannesburg). As the mines go deeper, labor needs increase; 100,000 men employed by 1899.

1896-1906   Final African risings and British victory over the Shona, Ndebele, Southern Tswana, Boers (Second Anglo-Boer War, 1899-1902), and finally the Zulu.

1906-'14   Ghandi leads passive resistance campaign for Indian civil rights.

1910   Union of South Africa unites Transvaal, Cape, Natal, and Orange Free State under Afrikaner nationalist government.

1911   Africans barred from skilled employment.

1912   South African Native National Congress, later to become African National Congress of South Africa (ANC S.A.), founded at Kimberley.

1913   Land Act defines limits of "native reserves" (present Bantustans).

1914-'18   South Africa enters World War I. "Die-hard" Afrikaners' revolt suppressed; German South-West Africa (Namibia) conquered.

1922   White miners revolt on Rand, crushed by alliance of Afrikaner nationalism and British mining capital.

1923   Urban Areas Act controls movement of Africans into towns.

1920s-'30s   Rise of the Industrial and Commercial Workers Union of Africa under Clements Kadalie; Mayibuye anti-pass campaign.

1930s-'40s   Afrikaner nationalism triumphant with high world gold price; "poor white" problem "solved" by confining prosperity to whites only.

1939-'45   South Africa enters World War II. Afrikaner nationalism split by pro-British and pro-German sympathies. (Vorster, among others, arrested for pro-German sabotage.) Protectionism and isolation due to war further stimulate development of manufacturing industries. Rapid urbanization of African workers.

1940s   Revival of African National Congress.

1944   *Sofazonke* ("Let us all die together") movement sets up shanty-town outside Orlando to protest lack of urban African housing.

1946   At least 60,000 African miners strike on Rand.

1948   "Purified" (anti-British) Afrikaner nationalism triumphs under Malan and Strijdom with Verwoerd as back-room boy.

1949   ANC Youth League adopts Programme of Action.

1950   Registration Act classifies people as white, Coloured or "Bantu." May 1: ANC general strike call; police shoot and 18 people die. Suppression of Communism Act—defining all attempts to change *status quo* as "communist"—is passed.

1951	Bantu Authorities Act defines power of chiefs in Bantustans. "Positive Apartheid" introduced.
1952	Defiance Campaign—black passive resistance movement against apartheid. Over 8000 demonstrators arrested.
1953-'55	Establishment of Bantu Education. "Dompass" introduced.
1956	Women's anti-pass campaign. Removals of Africans from the Johannesburg area started. 60,000 Coloureds removed from voting rolls in Cape Province, eliminating last black vote.
1956-'61	"Treason Trials": 156 leaders of ANC and allied movements arrested and tried under the Suppression of Communism Act.
1958	Verwoerd becomes Prime Minister.
1959	Luthuli, President of the ANC, banished. Pan-Africanist Congress forms under Sobukwe. Promotion of Bantu Self-Government Act passed, ruling that Africans may participate in government only in Bantustans.
1960	Sharpeville massacre—69 Africans killed by police while demonstrating peacefully. ANC and PAC banned (i.e. outlawed). Passes for African women put into effect. Government declares state of emergency, suspending the normal civil rights still extant; proclamation last several months.
1961	ANC and PAC decide upon military resistant; formation of military wings. (ANC's military arm is *Umkhonto we Sizwe*, "Spear of the Nation"; the PAC military wing is *POQO*, or "We Alone.")
1961-'64	Sabotage of electrical installations, municipal and Bantu Affairs offices.
1963	ANC leaders arrested, flee country or go underground. Seventeen underground leaders arrested at Rivonia. Ninety-day law (90 days detention in solitary, without trial) passed; 209 people listed as detained.
1964	Many sabotage arrests. Mandela, Sisulu, Mbeki and others sentenced to life imprisonment. Under 90-day law, 857 Africans arrested, 102 whites, 78 Indians and 58 Coloureds. First Transkei Legislative Assembly meets.
1966	Verwoerd assassinated; Vorster becomes Prime Minister.
1966-'72	Economic boom. High investments by U.S. and European corporations. Apartheid appears stabilized.
1968	Prohibition of political parties or gatherings by people of different races without a government permit.
1969	South African Students Organization (SASO) formed.
1971	Black People's Convention formed.
1973	100,000 African workers strike in various parts of country. Police shoot 14 African strikers dead at Carletonville gold mine.
1974	Liberation of Mozambique; pro-Frelimo rallies in South Africa.
1975	Government attacks Black Consciousness movement as subversive; arrest and trial of nine SASO leaders.
1975-'76	Angola wins independent from the Portuguese; fights Second War of

Liberation against invasion by South African, Zairese and FNLA troops; South African military humiliated.

1976   Soweto revolts. 649 people officially listed as shot dead by police. Thousands injured, arrested or detained.

1976-'77   Continuous unrest and suppression. Continued detention of potential opponents; more reports of torture and deaths of detainees. Several effective two-days "stay-aways"(general strikes). Boycott of schools to protest Bantu Education. Numerous schools, vehicles, administration offices and beerhalls burned. Organized African resistance and sabotage increased.

1977   Steve Biko, Honourary President of the BPC, killed in detention. The Soweto *World* newspaper, Christian Institute, SASO, South African Student Movement and BPC, among others, banned.

Appendix B: Demography

The South African government does not publish complete statistics for the African population, although it does publish them for the white, Coloured and Asian population. Those figures they do publish tend to be unreliable. For instance: when the riots in June 1976 started, the press reported the population of Soweto to be three quarters of a million, following official statistics. At the end of two months the same newspapers reported the population of Soweto at "nearly a million"; by the end of 1976 they had accepted that it was "almost one and a half million." There are no government figures published for income, employment, life expectancy or child mortality rates among Africans. One can only estimate such figures from surveys of particular areas, hospital records and market research studies.

Population(from the South African census estimate for mid-1975):

White:	4,274,000	(16.9%)
Colored:	2,432,000	(9%)
Asian:	734,000	(2.9%)
African:	17,823,000	(70.5%)

Life Expectancy Rates, 1967(in years):[1]

	Male	Female
White	64.6	70.1
Colored	44.8	47.8
Asian	55.8	54.8

For the African population, some idea of the comparative life expectancy rate can be gained from the following insurance company report, for urban areas only:

> If 100 blacks took out a life policy at age 15, only about 20 or even less will reach 60. This was not the case for whites. Here, the chances were that about 35 or over will reach the retiring age of 60.[2]

Two points should be noted: this report does not include rural areas, which have far worse mortality rates because of far worse medical facilities, and it does not include infant mortality rates.

Infant Mortality

In 1963, the infant mortality rate was officially 27 per thousand for whites; 200 per thousand for Africans in urban areas; and 300 to 400 per thousand for Africans in rural areas.[3]

The figures are no longer announced. However:

Infant mortality among African children has increased. Whereas in the 1960's the average annual death rate among 1 to 4 year olds was about 450 per 1000, in a survey in 1970 Professor John Reid found that, in the rural areas he investigated, infant mortality among African children was 25 times that of white children, i.e. 530 per 1000 ... 50 to 60 per cent of them die before the age of 5.[4]

(For comparison, in neighboring Botswana the infant mortality rates are: male, 103 per thousand, females, 91 per thousand.)

In a study of post mortem results from two hospitals, it was found that in 1975, of children under 10 who died in the only hospital for Africans in Durban (King Edward VIII Hospital), 30 per cent died as a direct result of malnutrition (kwashiorkor, etc.) In the whites- and Coloureds-only hospital (Addington Hospital), none of the white children died from malnutrition; among the Coloured patients, 8 per cent of the child deaths were from malnutrition.

Health Care:

Physician to Population Ratio, 1972[7]

White	Asian	Coloured	African
1:400	1:900	1:6200	1:44,000

Tuberculosis per thousand people, 1973[8]

White	Asian	Coloured	African
0.29	1.11	2.24	4.08

In the mines, white miners who develop T.B. are sent to a sanatorium at company expense until cured. Black miners are kept in bed two to three weeks and then sent home with antibiotics and the address of the nearest clinic.[9]

Education:

In 1974-5, approximately $190 million was spent on education for the African population. In the same period in excess of $750 million was spent on education for the white population.

Incomes per Capita:

The annual per capita African income was $245 in 1975, the annual per capita white income was $4200.[11]

1. Life expectancy rates announced in the House of Assembly by the Minister of Planning, 26th May, 1967. Cited in *Racial Discrimination* (Revised study, 1976), by H. Santa Cruz, United Nations, p. 191

2. Mr. W. Swart, quoted in the *World*, Aug. 10, 1977

3. House of Assembly debate, 1963; from *Racial Discrimination, op.cit.*, p. 191

4. *Land Tenure Conditions in South Africa,* United Nations Centre Against Apartheid, Notes and Documents, No. 37/76, Dec. 1976, p. 64

5. Botswana Census, 1971

6. *Implications of Apartheid on Health and Health Services in South Africa,* by "a group of black doctors in South Africa," United Nations Centre Against Apartheid, Notes and Documents No. 18/77, June 1977, p. 6

7. *Ibid.*, quoted from: *A Survey of Race Relations in South Africa, 1972*, South African Institute of Race Relations, 1973, p. 404

9. Francis Wilson, *Labour on the South African Gold Mines 1911-1969*, Cambridge University Press, London, 1972, p. 51

10. *Basic Facts on the Republic of South Africa and the Policy of Apartheid*, by Julian Friedman, United Nations Centre Against Apartheid, Notes and Documents No. 8/77, April 1977, p. 14.

11. *Ibid.*, p. 19

Appendix C: U.S. Investments

U.S. direct investment at year end, in millions of dollars:[1]

	1968	1976
In South Africa:	692	1,665
In manufacturing:	332	705
In rest of Africa:	981	2,802
In manufacturing:	68	257

In addition, U.S. companies make major investments through Canadian and European companies. If these investments could be traced, the total amount of U.S. investment in South Africa would be shown to be much higher.

In 1972, thirteen U.S. companies—including seven of the ten largest—controlled three quarters of U.S. investment in apartheid.

Name of South
African firm
Caterpillar (Africa)

Approximately three quarters of all U.S. investment in South Africa is controlled by 13 firms. Included in these 13 are seven of the ten largest industrial corporations in the U.S., among them: the auto companies, Ford, Chrysler and G.M.; the oil companies, Texaco, Standard Oil of California, and Mobil; and the electricity and electronics companies, ITT, General Electric, and IBM. Union Carbide, Caterpillar, and Minnesota Mining and Manufacturing (3M) are also included.

As the table above suggests, these companies have invested heavily in manufacturing in South Africa, which they have refused to do elsewhere in Africa. In this way they have made an important contribution to the apartheid regime, its economy and military.

Furthermore, U.S. banks—most notably, Chase Manhattan, Citibank, Morgan Guaranty and Manufacturers Hanover—have been very active recently in providing huge loans to the South African government. These loans have been especially useful to it in maintaining white minority rule in the current crisis, as it has faced a mounting capital outflow and balance of payments deficit.

1. U.S. Department of Commerce, *Survey of Current Business*, August 1976 and October 1969; and A. and N. Seidman, *U.S. Multinationals in Southern Africa*, Tanzanian Publishing House and Lawrence Hill, 1977

Notes

1. J.B. Vorster, quoted in R.W. Johnson, *How Long Will South Africa Survive?*, MacMillian Press Ltd., 1977, London, p. 182
2. Frederick Johnstone, "White Prosperity and White Supremacy in South Africa Today," in *African Affairs*, Vol. 69, No. 275, April 1970, p. 135
3. *Ibid., p. 130*
4. *Rand Daily Mail*, January 13, 1977
5. Ruth First, *The South African Connection*, Penguin Books, 1973, Harmondsworth, England, p. 30
6. Johnson, *op.cit.*, p. 269
7. A. Callinicos and J. Rogers, *Southern Africa After Soweto*, Pluto Press, London, 1977,p.159
8. B. Davidson, *Report on Southern Africa*, Jonathan Cape, 1952, London, p. 106
9. Ellen Kuzwayo, *Sash*, the Black Sash magazine, Vol. 18, No. 3, Nov. 1975, p. 7
10. Johnson, *op.cit.*, p. 189
11. *Rand Daily Mail*, extra, Aug. 27, 1976; the costs were later revised upwards to cope with inflation.
12. Wilson and Perrot, eds., *Outlook on a Century*, Lovedale and Spro-Cas Press, 1972, Cape, South Africa, p. 430
13. J. Campbell, *Travels in South Africa ... being a narrative of a second Journey, 1820*, Westley, 1822, London, Vol. I, p. 220
14. H. Bloom, P. Williams, T. Matshikiza, *King Kong*, Fontana Books, 1961, London, p. 44
15. *Sunday Tribune* (Durban), Aug. 14, 1977
16. *Ibid*
17. *Ibid*; also *World* (Johannesburg), Aug. 6, 1977
18. Johnson, *op.cit.*, p. 179
19. "Basic Economics," Lesson 8, People's College, *Weekend World* (Johannesburg), April 24, 1977
20. "Save the Starving Children," *Sunday Tribune* (Durban), June 27, 1976
21. E. Roux, *Time Longer Than Rope*, University of Wisconsin Press, 1966, p. 227
22. Mary Benson, *Struggle for a Birthright*, Penguin Books, 1966, Harmondsworth, England, p. 185
23. *Rand Daily Mail*, extra, Sept. 21, 1976
24. *Rand Daily Mail*, extra, Jan. 22, 1977
25. *Financial Mail* (Johannesburg), Oct. 15, 1976
26. T. Davenport, *South Africa, A Modern History*, MacMillian Press, 1977 London, p. 326

Further Reading

Poetry

Brutus, Dennis, *A Simple Lust*, Heinemann African Writers Series, 1973

Mtshali, Oswald Mbuyiseni, *Sounds of a Cowhid Drum*, Oxford University Press, London, 1975

Nortje, Arthur, *Dead Roots*, Heinemann African Writers Series, 1973

Serote, Mongane Wally, *Yakhal'inkomo*, Renoster Books, Johannesburg, 1974

Black Poets in South Africa, ed. Robert Royston, Heinemann African Writers Series, 1973

Poets to the People, International Defence and Aid for Southern Africa and Allen Unwin, 1975

Seven South African Poets, ed. Robert Royston, Heinemann African Writers Series, 1973

Novels

Abrahams, Peter, *Tell Freedom* (autobiography)

————*Mine Boy*, Heinemann African Writers Series

La Guma, Alex, *A Walk in the Night and other stories,* Heinemann African Writers Series

————*And a Threefold Cord*, Heinemann African Writers Series

————*The Stone Country*, Seven Seas Publishing House

————*In the Fog at the Season's End,* Heinemann African Writers Series

Mphahlele, Ezekial, *Down Second Avenue*

————, *In Corner B*

Themba, Can, *The Will to Die*, Heinemann African Writers Series

Zwelonke, D.M., *Robben Island*, Heinemann African Writers Series

Plays

H. Bloom, P. Williams, T. Matshikiza, *King Kong*, Fontana Books, 1961

Fugard, A., Kani, J., Ntshona, W., *Statements* (includes "Sizwe Bansi is Dead," "The Island",and "The Bloodknot").

General Reading

Benson, Mary, *The Struggle for a Birthright* (Penguin Books, 1966) Story of the formation and struggles of the African National Congress of South Africa from 1912 to 1966.

Bunting, Brian, *Rise of the South African Reich* (Penguin, 1970) Details the establishment of apartheid and its roots.

Callinicos, A. and Rogers, J., *South Africa After Soweto* (Pluto Press, 1977)

Cope, Jack, *House of Bondage*, a photographic study of black urban life in South Africa in the 1960s.

Davenport, T.R.H., *South Africa, A Modern History* (Cambridge University Press, 1977) The only up-to-date scholarly synthesis of South African history over the last two centuries.

Davidson, Basil, Slovo, Joe, and Wilkinson, Anthony, *Southern Africa: The New Politics of Revolution* (Penguin African Library, 1976) Articles on Angola, South Africa and Zimbabwe today—excellent.

Desmond, Cosmos, *The Discarded People, An Account of African Resettlement in* *South Africa* (Penguin, 1971) A priest's eye-witness account of the hardships of re-settlement in Natal.

First, R., Steel, J., Gurney, C., *The South African Connection, Western Investment in* *Apartheid* (Penguin, 1973) An investigation of international, especially British, economic support for apartheid.

Johnson, R.W., *How Long Will South Africa Survive?* (MacMillian Press, 1977) The real-politik of South Africa's international position today.

LeMay, G.H.L., *Black and White in South Africa* (MacDonald, Library of the 20th Century, 1971) A brief, well-illustrated history of South Africa, concentrating on apartheid and resistance to apartheid.

Luthuli, Albert, *Let My People Go* (Meridian Books, 1970) The autobiography of the most important black South African leader of the 1950s and early '60s.

Mandela, Nelson, *No Easy Walk to Freedom* (Heinemann African Writers Series)

Palmer, R., and Parsons, Q.N., eds., *Roots of Rural Poverty in Central and Southern* *Africa* (Heinemann, 1977) Scholarly historical studies of the stimulation and de-struction of peasant communities under colonialism in southern Africa.

Seidman, A. and N., *U.S. Multinationals in Southern Africa* (Tanzanian Publishing House and Lawrence Hill, Conn., 1977) U.S. investment in apartheid and South African expansionism in southern Africa.

Wilson, Francis, *Labour on the South African Gold Mines, 1911-1969* (Cambridge University Press, 1972) Historical analysis of the position of the worker in the South African gold mines, resulting in the present socio-economic position of the African miner.

Counter Information Services, *Black South Africa Explodes,* Anti-Report No. 17, London. The events of 1976 and the conditions that caused them.